The Legal Stuff

Copyright © 2021 by Cary Jack - The Happy Hustle

All rights reserved. No part of this publication may be reproduced in whole or in part, or transmitted in any form by any means electronic, mechanical, magnetic, and photographic including photocopying, recording or by any information storage and retrieval system without prior written permission by the publisher, except for the brief inclusions of quotations in a review. This work is intended as an aide to self-improvement only. This book does not seek to give medical advice and is not a substitute for licensed medical care. Readers shall hold harmless the author and publisher for any events or actions that arise from the reading of or attempts to implement the methods in this book. Neither is any liability assumed for damages resulting from the use of the information contained herein. Note that this material is subject to change without notice.

ISBN: 978-0-578-97719-5

Cover Design by Jason Lefrock, Studio 217

Edited By: Charles Serabian & Megan Kendzior

Happy Publishing INC

TheHappyHustle.com

THE HAPPY HUSTLE

This book was written to help you put the Happy in your Hustle and live a blissfully balanced life you love, one full of passion, purpose, and positive impact.

SHOUT OUTS

Shout out to my ma, for taking this thing to the finish line with years of editing and feedback. You rock. Love ya.

To my brother, business partner, and best friend Grant for always being my ride or die. Here's to positively changing the world together.

To my beautiful lova Steph, for supporting the Happy Hustle since inception the late-night writing benders and weekend cabin getaways. I love and cherish you and couldn't be more grateful to be doing life together.

To my sister Megan, for being unapologetically you and standing up for what you believe in. Thank you for doing the final editing pass and making this a better book.

To my dad, for instilling wisdom and work ethic. Thanks for being there.

To my cousin Jason, founder of Studio 217 who did the front and back cover design, the Happy Hustle logo, swag, you name it, the guy has been my go-to for branding and is a rockstar. Thanks, primo.

To my amazing Happy Hustle team, especially Connie who formatted the whole book, y'all rock.

To all of my family and friends who have supported the Happy Hustle in ways both big and small, you know who you are.

And to YOU, who this book is truly for. Allow this to help you put the Happy in your Hustle for life. I am so grateful for you reading this!

TABLE OF CONTENTS

Intro'ing The Happy Hustle……………………………………………………..1

Alignment 1: Selfless Service… ……………………………………...……..21

Alignment 2: Optimized Health………………………………………….…..28

Alignment 3: Unplug Digitally……………………………………………….40

Alignment 4: Loving Relationships…………………………………...……..47

Alignment 5: Mindful Spirituality……………………………………………61

Alignment 6: Abundance Financially………………………………………..74

Alignment 7: Personal Development………………………………………..87

Alignment 8: Passionate Hobbies………………………………………….102

Alignment 9: Impactful Work……………………………………………….110

Alignment 10: Nature Connection………………………………………….124

Bonus Alignment: Blissful Balance ……………………………………….132

Bringin' it all together………………………………………………………141

INTRO'ING THE HAPPY HUSTLE

Ultimate freedom. Financial abundance. Loving relationships. Everyday fulfillment. Blissful balance. That is what this book is all about.

Welcome to The Happy Hustle™, my friend! First things first, I want to establish that this isn't your average step-by-step, "I will show you how to…" blah blah, BS self-help book. So, if you don't mind tossing those expectations out the window right meow, that would be a great starting point. Real talk: this book was drafted to not just tell you, but to teach you. To not just be words on a page, but to cut through life's noise and speak to your soul. To provide you with a road map, a system, a way, to Happy Hustle a blissfully balanced life of passion, purpose, and a positive impact. This book includes Actionable Takeaways and Happy Hustle Hacks (plus a ton more resources) that you can immediately implement to enrich your reality.

I didn't spend 2 ½ years writing this for shits and gigs. I want it to mean something to you. You will legit be able to pick it up, flip it open to any page, and get real value. You will be able to go back and reread it when you drift off, out of alignment, and need a reminder. See, I fully realize you are busy and have roughly an eight-second attention span. Heck, you've probably already lost focus and thought about three other things and we're only on the first page.

You see, **balance = happiness**, amigo. And I promise you, if you stay with me to the end, this book can help you achieve blissful balance and avoid burnout while ultimately changing your life in the best way. Well technically, this book isn't going to do shit for your life. You absorbing the content and implementing the **S.O.U.L.M.A.P.P.I.N.™** system (don't worry we'll get into it) is what's gonna do it for you. You gotta take action. You gotta take accountability for your reality. Are you game? Stop reading if not. Happy Hustlers are always honest with themselves. So, if you are out, that's cool, I've still got love for you and wish you nothing but the best. However, if you are in, meaning ready to commit to finishing this book and taking massive action throughout the process, then let's fucking go! (Please excuse my language throughout in advance, the truth is -- I'm fired up to share this with you and wrote it how I would say it to you in person over an ice-cold brewski.)

Chances are you're not where you want to be. You're hustlin', but not happy.

Allow me to go out on multiple depressing limbs here and take a stab at where you may be at in your current reality. Let me know if any (or all) of these resonate with you:

- You want more fulfillment and meaning in your life but you don't make time to volunteer for causes you believe in or selflessly serve others. You've been living largely for yourself, in pursuit of personal gain rather than focusing on helping others in need.

- You don't have the body, brain, flexibility, recovery, or performance you know is possible but you don't exercise regularly or implement healthy habits like eating a nutritious diet. Or if you regularly exercise and eat healthy, you know you're not even close to reaching the full potential of your optimized self.

- You spend too much time on your laptop, or on your phone scrolling social media, or watching pointless tv shows or movies and not living in the present moment. You know you need a digital detox as you can recognize you have a low-key tech addiction but can't seem to escape the dopamine dumps.

- You don't have the loving, pleasure-filled personal relationship you desire and your overall connection to your family is lacking and/or "complicated." There's adversity and issues in the relationship realm, mainly caused by working too much and not giving enough energy and attention to your loved ones.

- You know you should meditate or have a mindfulness practice of some sort because you realize almost all of the most successful people in the world do, but you don't because you have too much shit to do in your schedule, and there's just no time for 10 minutes a day for inner work.

- You don't have the bank account you desire and are struggling to make ends meet, let alone pay off the student loan and credit card debt you have accrued. Or maybe you do have some $$ in the bank but you don't have an actual system to spend, save, and invest that is guaranteed to result in financial abundance.

- You know you should be reading and investing in your personal growth but you choose to binge-watch meaningless shows on Netflix or scroll on social media for hours comparing and despairing to other people's lives instead of learning new skills and absorbing valuable content.

- You want to have more fun and enjoy hobbies regularly like potentially taking up a martial art, dance lessons or oil-painting but you feel guilty whenever you do anything for yourself as you have other very important things to accomplish, like doing the job you don't like.

- You feel stuck doing a job you deep down hate (or dislike), that lacks purpose. You want to be your own boss and have your own business but you are shackled to your comfortable, secure yet unsatisfying work. And if you are your own boss, you are currently hustlin' but not happy. Working your face off and out of balance. Prioritizing profits & success over faith, family, friends, fitness, fun, etc.

- You spend the majority of your time indoors, under man-made toxic blue lights, breathing recycled air, getting beamed by electromagnetic frequencies (EMFs), or commuting in your vehicle and not nearly enough time in nature connecting to Mother Earth and your environment. You love being around animals in nature but don't make enough time to get outside and tap into your true primal nature. Ultimately, you feel stressed with numerous never-ending responsibilities you created for yourself, and even when you do accomplish all those things, it's never enough. You are out of balance and barely have any time for yourself.

Whew, that was a lot. Any of those hit home? Good. I wanted to lay it all out there early in this mofo and be real with you. Now you have to be real with me by being real with yourself (say what?). Which bullet above is the biggest pain point in your current reality? Make a mental note because each bullet above (represents what I call an Alignment) and its remedy will be covered in the pages to follow. I am going to address each and show you how to Happy Hustle in all areas of life. Now you may be saying to yourself, "Cary, who the hell are you to show me the promised land?"

Well, I may not have all the answers, but I do have some. People often ask me how I have escaped the 9-5 grind and live a purposeful and prosperous life on my terms while getting paid to do the things I love to do. All the while juggling three successful business ventures, hosting a top 1% global podcast based on downloads (The Happy Hustle Podcast), being a professional model/actor, and creating inspiring and educational content that positively impacts millions of lives. Not to mention I travel the world (pending there's no global pandemic with travel restrictions), enjoy hobbies regularly like fly fishing and martial arts, make a global ecological impact, and consistently show up as the best lover, brother, son, dog dad (and soon to be real dad) I can be, while giving back to others every chance I get. And I do all that while making money as I sleep with systematized online businesses, leveraging my time most efficiently and effectively.

Now, let me be straight up, as I will be throughout this book's entirety, I am still on my journey, Happy Hustlin' towards my glorious grand vision, and am constantly in search of self-development in the process. Nonetheless, I am happy. I am happy within the hustle and live an amazingly blessed life. And you can too. Wherever you are and wherever you're going, the Happy Hustle is the way. However, it wasn't always this way for me.

See, before I was Happy Hustlin', I was just hustlin'. As a former NYC tech-entrepreneur who fell victim to the ever-growing entrepreneurial burnout, I now know the importance of balance. I was working 100+ hour weeks, getting roughly 5 hours of sleep, and grindin' my face off. All for-profit and success. It wasn't until I actually landed the 7-figure VC funding deal and partnerships with Microsoft and IBM for our innovative tech startup, that I realized I was unhappy and unfulfilled. So after many tears and a hard conversation with my brother, business, and best friend, I made a massive pivot. We said no to the funding, folded the company, and moved to Bangkok, Thailand for 10 months. It was there where I figured out a better way to work and live. A way to have my cake and eat it too. A way to find happiness within the hustle. That is where Happy Hustle was born. And this book signifies the replicable journey that anyone struggling with imbalance and unhappiness can emulate to transform their reality into a blissfully balanced life they love.

Within these pages, I share my proprietary framework, which I call the 10 Alignments. Think of these as life's curriculum to achieving an A+ everyday reality. Not much for school analogies? Me either. So rather think of these as a blueprint to building your dream home. Or a road map to your perfect utopia. Whatever you want to think of these as just know that these 10 Alignments are the way to Happy Hustle your dream reality.

It's like baking a cake. To bake a delicious carrot cake (my favorite cake) from scratch, you need the proper ingredients in the correct quantities. Sure, it's still edible if you leave out the almonds and don't use enough baking powder but then it's not carrot cake and you're settling for something less. Where are you settling in your life? Where are you missing ingredients? Where are you lacking passion and purpose?

I don't want you eating sub-par cake any longer my friend. You got one life to live (at least in this body) so live it fully! Ok, I broke down this book and life as a Happy Hustler into separate Alignments (ingredients). It's time to gather all of the proper ingredients so you can make the most delectable, enjoyable, heavenly cake beyond all of your wildest dreams.

These are the 10 Alignments of a Happy Hustler which make up the acronym **S.O.U.L.M.A.P.P.I. N™**

1) **S**elfless Service
2) **O**ptimized Health
3) **U**nplug Digitally
4) **L**oving Relationships
5) **M**indful Spirituality
6) **A**bundance Financially
7) **P**ersonal Development
8) **P**assionate Hobbies
9) **I**mpactful Work
10) **N**ature Connection

Now you may have read the above ingredient list and thought to yourself, "I am definitely missing a few." Well fear not, you can actually identify which ingredients you may be lacking at **www.thehappyhustle.com/assessment!** This 2-minute assessment will show you exactly where your life (and baking game) stands. I promise I'll be done with this cake analogy soon.

Stick with me as I attempt to write us out of it. But in reality, even if you did have all the ingredients, do you have the proper quantities of each? Not enough carrots and you might as well have a flour cake, which is not as delicious or nutritious.

Furthermore, if you're not a master baker, you're probably going to need some baking instructions to know how to put it all together. Let's say you do somehow throw all of the ingredients together in forcible fashion but forget to turn on the oven, you're going to end up with sweet brown goo-poo delight. Comprende the importance of not missing a step? I love my Latina so excuse me as I speak Spanglish throughout, lo siento (sorry). I also used to live in Barcelona and picked up the lingo abroad. Speaking of instructions, the 5 Stages to Happy Hustlin' is your go-to baking guide for a sweet life. You can use the 5 stages to increase your score in each of the 10 Alignments in order to go from whatever score you're currently at to a 5... if you didn't take the assessment yet don't worry more on this later.

Apply The 5 Stages to Happy Hustlin' in each Alignment:

1) *Do an honest audit of your reality and feel gratitude for where you are.*

2) *Define your vision for success, what does a 5 look like in this Alignment?*

3) *Reverse engineer the process and create a winning game plan.*

4) *Take massive action and execute! Manage your time & priorities accordingly.*

5) *Persistent consistency. Enjoy the Journey Happy Hustlin' a life of passion, purpose, and positive impact.*

These stages will help you identify where you are and what you're missing. No matter if you're in a job you hate or lacking health and wealth, The 5 Stages to Happy Hustlin' will help you create a plan in each of the 10 Alignments and turn your ingredients into the delicious masterpiece you deserve.

If you're feeling overwhelmed by the 10 Alignments and the 5 Stages of Happy Hustlin' we've covered thus far, fear not. We will explore each in-depth and the application of this framework in the pages to follow so stick with me, partner.

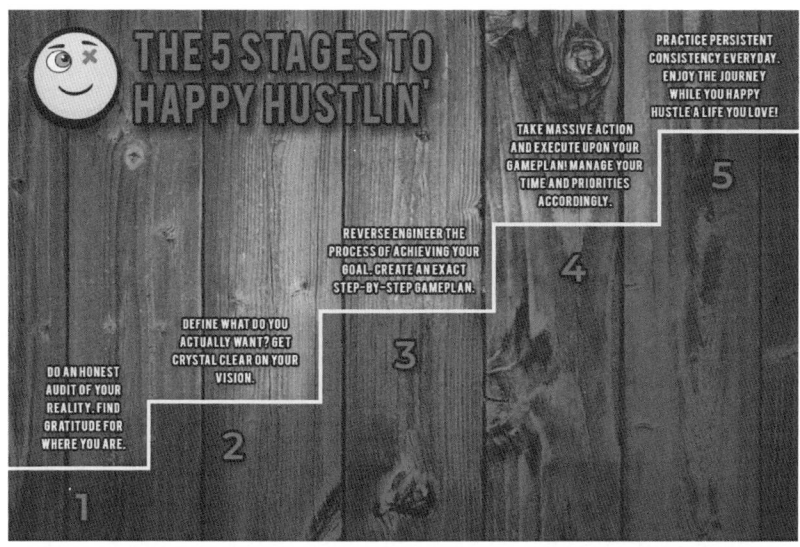

The Happy Hustle is how you can wake up excited to carpe diem and live a life you love while still striving for more. You have the ingredients and the instructions, now the real key to happiness is having balance. Fear not, I will show you how I balance each Alignment using the proprietary **S.O.U.L.M.A.P.P.I.N.™** system and bake each to perfection (most of the time) and how you can too. So, raise your whisk if you're ready to bake! (said no one ever, c'mon Cary - no more baking references). But for real, it's going to get a whole lot cream cheesier so just prepare now.

It is time for you to Happy Hustle your dream reality. And don't just do it for yourself. Do it for the world. The world is in dire need of your unapologetic self to step into its full potential and share your message. It yearns for the positive change that will come from it.

More so now than ever in history, we must use the power of business as a force for good to solve global issues. We all have the power to make a positive impact. We can use our Happy Hustles to serve the greater good and humanity at large. **Author's note:** I fully realize I just went from using baking puns to a serious save the world tone.

You truly can create financial abundance for yourself and your loved ones without doing so negatively at the Earth's or other people's expense. We can utilize sustainable practices while respecting natural resources. Individually, we can consciously make choices that collectively will change the world. It's time to Happy Hustle in alignment with your true self's desires while simultaneously serving a cause(s) that speaks to your soul. You can live a life of passion, purpose, and positive impact while being blissfully balanced and we're going to get into how, so buckle up y'all, it's go time!

STORY TIME: FROM DITCH DIGGER TO SMOOTHIE CHEF, THE NOTEWORTHY HUSTLES THAT MADE ME...

I feel it's only right to give you a little backstory on who the heck I am.

I've been a hustler since a very early age. My siblings and I were taught that if you want something, you have to earn it. I am the product of two entrepreneurial parents: My mother, a chiropractor with her own, thriving practice, and my father, a mechanic by trade who owned a busy repair shop and automotive parts business. I learned first-hand what it took to run your own business and the work ethic necessary to be successful. Both earned modest middle-class income which allowed us to have our basic needs met. I didn't have the easiest of childhood (but it could have been a lot worse) as my early years were filled with a rough divorce, family illness, emotional and physical abuse, and moving 24 times before the age of 18. Nonetheless, I did have love and support from both parents.

My father was strict. He was an "old-school" man of discipline. He had 6 siblings and left home when he was 16. He grew up hardened by his circumstances. He carved his path and intended for us to do the same. My mom lost her mother at an early age to cancer. Her father was busy running a fine men's wear store and was a part of the Freemason society. As a consequence, he wasn't around much for her throughout her childhood.

She had to hustle to make it on her own, as did my father. My entrepreneurial mentality was forged due to my environment and naturally translated to hungry ambition. But no worries if your parents were not entrepreneurs, or around for that matter, I am going to show you how you can always find a way to achieve what you set out for. Hang in there on this quick trip down memory lane so you know where I'm coming from.

Here is a list of the random activities I've done in exchange for money:

Lawn Mower – My first real dollar earned was done so by cutting the neighbors' lawn. Oh, the sweet smell of fresh-cut grass still brings me back...

Lemonade Stander - Slangin' juice to the locals and passersby in the neighborhood.

Construction Worker - Digging ditches = calloused hands.

Smoothie Barista (at Smoothie King) - Consistency is key with any great smoothie. Side note: This was the first job I was hired and fired in the same week.

Soccer Trainer/Camp Counselor - Being a pretty decent player myself, I started first working as a trainer to the youngsters then actually created my own soccer camp business which pulled in a couple of g's a summer in my early teens. Loved teaching the youth and especially enjoyed playing "hitters and dodgers" where you line the kids up and beam balls at them while they attempt to dodge, thus occasionally pegging one or two of them off their feet... don't worry they loved it and no one sustained any permanent injuries.

Coach Cary in action.

Ice Cream Scooper (Coldstone Creamery) - Where I would sing for tips and wore my first (and not last) banana suit.

Sanitarian Technician (a.k.a dishwasher) – Talk about pruney fingers.

Expo Chef – Making house salads like nobody's business.

Bus Boy – Where I mastered the art of carrying multiple plates at one time.

Restaurant Server – Understanding customers' non-verbal communication and body language is essential for top tips.

Flair Bartender – Dancing on top of the bar was the norm, also when and where I realized the entertainment value of shaking drinks in silly ways boosted tips exponentially. I enjoyed my time bartending and even got to travel around to various parties all over the world just to mix drinks and perform... my go to cocktail was the Old Fashioned.

Getting flown down to bartend at the Corona Sunsets party on the beach in the Dominican Republic didn't suck.

Smoothie Barista (Round 2- Jamba Juice) – Wheatgrass and oatmeal were perks of the job, also this is where I wore my second banana suit - legit a full body banana suit with face and armholes.

Distributor – Mainly for goods that were previously illegal, taught me the value of supply and demand economics. Won't get into this one too much ;)

Italian Restaurant Server/Bartender – Specialty cocktails began to be a thing this time so I started learning mixology.

WGN News Network – News anchor internship in college (not paid but gained experience).

Comcast SportsNet – T.V. sportscaster internship in college (not paid but gained experience).

Nightlife Party Host/Promoter – One of the best jobs I ever had. Literally, got paid to party.

Male Dancer – Yes, use your imagination. Think of a less choreographed version of Magic Mike ;).

Catering Worker – Serving/bartending for catered upscale events, where made a ton of contacts with the 1% and would often eat the untouched leftovers off people's plates. Hey, I was hungry.

Brand Ambassador – Representing and promoting some of the largest brands in the world at pop-up events (Hermes, Burberry, Topman, D-Squared, Ted Baker).

Promo-Model – More casual gigs, smiling and being personable in clothes of all sorts usually for larger-scale events (Neiman Marcus, Saks 5th Avenue, Nordstrom).

Professional Model – Formal bookings, I got paid to have my image taken usually for magazine, internet, or video publications (Lifetime Fitness, City Furniture, Cadillac, too many to list). At one point, I was represented by some of the top talent agencies in the world, Wilhelmina and Next Models.

Clean shaven Cary doesn't come out too often anymore, but here's a headshot from when he did.

Professional Commercial Actor – Formal commercial bookings where I would often play characters while promoting various nation-wide brands (Corona, Home Depot, Jeep, Allegra, Tire Kingdom, Mich Ultra, etc. You can see my professional reel at www.caryjack.com/actin).

Soccer Coach – Actually got certified to officially coach. #1 goal, keep every kid alive, but in all seriousness, I always enjoyed teaching the beautiful game to young players.

International Tour Guide – This was actually a dream job. My brother and I spent over 100+ hours learning Portuguese, building our resumes, creating a video to submit, etc., all to land a job in Rio De Janeiro, Brazil for the 2014 World Cup. 4 months of paid pure pleasure was to follow.

Start-Up Entrepreneur – This was my title for a hot minute, roughly 8 years as I started and stopped 4 legit companies #failingforward all the while. I love business and using it as a force for good but it took me a while to figure it out.

Grant & I had some of the best times of our life in Rio de Janeiro, Brazil while working a dream job during the 2014 World Cup.

Website Developer – I managed and built a couple of websites in my day for some quick cash. I am now grateful for the experience as I have leaned on it while building my own biz and helping advise others with their online presence.

Online Entrepreneur – The digital age is upon us friends, I have created and sold courses, e-books, audio products, podcasts, digital products, masterminds, and more on a variety of topics from modeling to self-improvement to sales to fitness and randomness in between. Love being location independent and being able to work from anywhere with a Wi-Fi connection.

Biohacking Health Coach – diving deep down the rabbit hole of human optimization, I've helped clients from Olympic Gold Medal Athletes to Fortune 500 CEOs to soccer moms all over the world optimize their mind, body, and spirit using a mixture of ancient wisdom and modern science.

Online Salesman – I sold over 1 million dollars over Zoom calls from 2019 - 2021 working typically less than 20 hours a week and have continued growing sales volume year after year ever since. Sales are the lifeblood of any business and I happen to love the art of the deal. Want to make more money? Get good at sales. More on this later.

Co-Founder of Start-Ups – I have created multiple businesses with my brother and currently am fighting the plastic pollution epidemic and climate change while using our business (www.ecobreakthroughs.com) as a force for good.

Marketing Copywriter – One of the more valuable skills any entrepreneur could learn and implement. Copywriting is all around you everywhere. Using words to inspire action in all of your content is non-negotiable in business. I've done this for myself and other companies. The point being: learn how to write copy that converts.

Podcast Host – Host of the 5 star rated, top 1% podcast globally, The Happy Hustle Podcast where I interview high-performing entrepreneurs, spiritual gurus, and world-class Happy Hustlers who are living a life of passion, purpose, and positive impact while manifesting their dream reality and how you can too! If you haven't already, I highly suggest checking it out, available on all podcast platforms. #shamelessplug

Author – hence this book :) which has been a real labor of love, let me tell ya'.

Personal Brand & Sales Strategist – I worked with an awesome company called Brand Builders Group who helps individuals turn their reputation into revenue. I started as a client, building my own personal brand under their guidance, and now have helped others using their transformative system to launch, grow, and monetize. This is an example of creating a strategic partnership that is truly a win-win-win. Side note: Strategic partnerships are one of the fastest ways to expedite your success and increase your income.

Happy Hustler – a lifestyle entrepreneur living a life of passion, purpose, and positive impact while maintaining blissful balance and helping others do the same!

I know, quite the list ... lots of lessons learned! And for the record, I fully realize I have been blessed from birth compared to much of the world, by just being born a white male in the USA, which I do not take for granted whatsoever, yet, it was still a humbling journey to get here!

ACTIONABLE TAKEAWAY

I share that laundry list of past gigs to show you that **it doesn't matter where you've been, or where you are, it matters where you're headed and what you are willing to do to get there.** As long as you keep going and improving every day, work is work. We all gotta eat. We all gotta keep the lights on. It's a part of life, and especially as a Happy Hustler, you do whatever it takes. It's a part of the process.

That said, don't let your current work dictate your joy. If you're not happy with what you're doing, that's ok. Sometimes you have to do things you don't necessarily want to. We all do. Sometimes that means wearing a banana suit, shoveling shit, answering phones, going door-to-door selling things, serving food, fill in the blank. The act of hustlin' to make money and pursue financial freedom (aka life on your terms) will keep you humble and hungry, I know it has done so for me. Here's a quote by yours truly that sums up my mentality: "You have to earn the right to do what you love."

I found out quite early on in my life that I wasn't a good employee. It's not that I don't like the concept of being an employee and learning from others, but for some reason, I would tend to discover what I deemed a better, more efficient way of doing my "job" or the task at hand. I would end up doing it my way, and employers don't seem to like employees who do things "their own way," even if I felt my way was more efficient and effective. So, I decided to work freelance gigs, odd jobs, and hustle. Working odd jobs meant that I could decide when and how I worked. However, it's definitely not the most "secure" way of living because you never really know where your next check is coming from, but I wouldn't have it any other way! Ok, maybe I would have it, so someone just pays me to hang out with them. Only kidding, I like the fact that I only eat what I earn. No one said being an entrepreneur came with job security.

All of the ridiculous random jobs that have paid me in some form of compensation are a part of my journey. From free food from catering jobs, to free products from promo-modeling, to free experiences from being a brand ambassador, to free lessons from business colleagues, I would soak up whatever I could from every opportunity. Not to mention rubbing elbows with the "elite" and expanding my network all the while (I always engaged in conversations regardless of my uniform). Each job comes with some form of payment in addition to the monetary component so take stock in what you're doing right now for money and discover value in other mediums.

I look for the positive with each hustlin' endeavor and do my best to make as many connections throughout the process; many of which have translated to lifelong mutually beneficial connections.

Opportunities come from all angles. Whether bartending or digging ditches, I am grateful for this roller-coaster of a ride. Earning my way Happy Hustlin', staying humble and hungry. Now before we go any further, I got a bone to pick with you.

One of the gigs I enjoyed greatly was working as a Biohacking Health Coach for amazing entrepreneurs and athletes. But it was especially rad working with these badass hockey players, Jonathan Toews & Duncan Keith. Both multiple time Olympic Gold Medalists and Stanley Cup winners who are the best of the best at what they do as well as super cool and kind dudes.

DA ASSESSMENT: THIS SETS THE FOUNDATION FOR YOUR HAPPY HUSTLIN' JOURNEY

If you breezed over the initial Happy Hustler Assessment call to action (www.thehappyhustle.com/assessment), here it is again, only you can't escape it as I put it in the book – muahahaha! Let's identify where you're at in your life, and where you may be lacking, shall we? One of the ways that we can first quantify this is by going through a quick assessment. I want you to get real tangible value right from the get-go with this book. That means you're going to have to do some self-quantification.

So, let's start by measuring where you rank in each of the 10 Alignments of a Happy Hustler aka the S.O.U.L.M.A.P.P.I.N.™ acronym. Be honest with yourself here. Remember, that what you measure, you can manage.

Now I wasn't much for school but I do know the grading scale. As you go through the following questions, score yourself in each of the 10 Alignments using this rubric:

10 Alignments Score Rubric:

5 – **A:** *Crushing it & Happy Hustlin!*
4 – **B:** *Satisfied & Making Progress*
3 – **C:** *Ok & Getting By*
2 – **D:** *Slackin' & Need to Step It Up*
1 – **F:** *Significantly Lacking & Must Prioritize Change In This Area*

1) *Do you practice Selfless Service?* Do you help causes and people who need it? Do you volunteer and donate to others who are less fortunate? Or have you been living more for yourself and not making time to give? (Measure where you rank in this area 1-5, write it in your journal or on your note-taking device).

2) *Do you have Optimized Health?* Do you have the body and mind you desire? Do you exercise and eat healthy daily? Or maybe you are not where you want to be... (Measure where you rank in this area 1-5, write it in your journal or on your note-taking device)

3) *How often do you Unplug Digitally?* Do you regularly do digital detoxes? Are you putting your phone on airplane mode, closing the laptop, turning off the tv, and tapping into your own thoughts? Do you have tech restriction rules (ie: no tech 60 min in the morning and 60 min before bed) and the daily discipline to adhere to each? (Measure where you rank in this area 1-5, write it in your journal or on your note-taking device)

4) *Do you have Loving Relationships with your family and friends?* Is there plentiful pleasure and love with your significant other? Or maybe there is pain and angst? (Measure where you rank in this area 1-5, write it in your journal or on your note-taking device)

5) *Do you practice Mindful Spirituality?* Are you connected to a higher power? Do you meditate and have an attitude of gratitude? Or maybe you feel disconnected and lack meaning? (Measure where you rank in this area, write it in your journal or on your note-taking device.)

6) *Are you Abundant Financially?* Do you spend, save, and invest wisely? Or are you living paycheck to paycheck and living in fear of your finances? (Measure where you rank in this area, write it in your journal or on your note-taking device)

7) *How often do you focus on Personal Development?* Are you regularly reading, listening, and watching educational and inspiring content? Or maybe not so much... maybe you're binging Netflix more than you know you should. (Measure where you rank in this area 1-5, write it in your journal or on your note-taking device).

8) *Do you have Passionate Hobbies you do regularly?* Do you have fun and participate in activities you enjoy? Or do you skip doing things for yourself because you often feel you're too busy... (Measure where you rank in this area 1-5, write it in your journal or on your note-taking device).

9) *Do you currently have Impactful Work or a career that fills you with joy and fulfillment?* Do you feel you are working in alignment with your higher calling? Or maybe you feel stuck, unsatisfied with what you do for a living, and are craving change? (Measure where you rank in this area 1-5, write it in your journal or on your note-taking device)

10) *Do you have Nature Connection?* Do you regularly get outside and tap into your true primal self and Mother Earth? Or do you spend most of your time indoors on your devices, soaking up man-made light, breathing in recycled air? (Measure where you rank in this area 1-5, write it in your journal or on your note-taking device)

See that wasn't so bad! Now, tally up your total score by adding each of the 10 scores together. If you are below a 36, you are not yet a Happy Hustler. That means you ranked yourself below a 4 or a 5 in one if not more of the 10 Alignments.

If you are 37 or above, then congrats! This means you are currently a Happy Hustler! Yahoo!

However, we can all improve, so let's not get complacent. Read this book in its entirety and determine what you can do to increase your score even more! There are levels to this game, fam.

See, I like to measure myself using this assessment once a week, on Sunday evening usually. I'll rank myself on the past week and then prioritize and/or change accordingly for the week ahead. I suggest you do the same, as we are constantly evolving and need regular, consistent weekly measurements in each Alignment in order to accurately course correct on our Happy Hustle journey. I know it seems repetitive but you know what else is also repetitive and very necessary? Showering and wiping your ass. So you do it. Treat this similarly.

Again, if you would like to take the most updated version of the Happy Hustler Assessment online and get your scores sent directly to you, go to **www.happyhustle.com/assessment.**

Pro tip: I like to save it as a favorite on my browser so I can easily take it each week.

I know you are hungry for more in your life. I know you are a learner and someone who wants to become a better version of yourself or else you wouldn't be reading this. The best way to do that is by continuously quantifying where you are and where you want to go. The 5 Stages to Happy Hustlin' in each Alignment will show you how to transform a 1 ranking to a 5 in each Alignment, here they are again:

The 5 Stages to Happy Hustlin' in each Alignment:

1) Do an honest audit of your reality and feel gratitude for where you are.

2) Define your vision for success, what does a 5 look like in this Alignment?

3) Reverse engineer the process and create a winning game plan.

4) Take massive action and execute! Manage your time & priorities accordingly.

5) Persistent consistency. Enjoy the journey while Happy Hustlin' a life of passion, purpose, and positive impact.

If you don't already have a Blissful Balancer, and want help Happy Hustlin' and keeping yourself accountable to a blissfully balanced life, then I HIGHLY recommend picking up one of our Happy Hustle Blissful Balancer fridge magnets. This whiteboard fridge magnet goes on your refrigerator door (no duh Cary) and is a constant reminder of the daily action tasks you need to complete in each of the 10 Alignments in order to blissfully balance your day, thus your week, and thus your life. This isn't a ploy to get you to purchase more shit from me. This was specifically created to actually help you implement the S.O.U.L.M.A.P.P.I.N.™ system into your daily life. I made it analog by design, meaning not an app or tech tool, and that was specifically to help get you off your devices and back to the present moment. It really can make a positive difference when utilized consistently.

Get a Blissful Balancer at www.thehappyhustle.com/hub!
Or scan this QR code:

This tool is a game-changer and was specifically designed to parlay with this book to Happy Hustle your blissfully balanced dream reality. Take advantage of this unique tool and even consider ordering one for your significant other, friends, and family as the benefits are exponential.

And no, you don't need to read the book first as it comes with separate instructions, although the book is definitely recommended. And if you're ballin' on a budget currently, you can just print out a new PDF each week and tape it on your fridge for FREE.

Remember what you can measure, you can manage. Measure your balance because balance equals happiness, my friend. You're probably going to get sick of me saying that but I bet you'll remember it by the end of the book. ;)

Blissful Balancer instructions:

So rather than making you wait to finish the book, I want you to start Happy Hustlin' right away. If you have a Blissful Balancer, amazing! If not, you're going to want to, you can get one here: **www.thehappyhustle.com/hub**

Here are the step-by-step instructions on how to use the Blissful Balancer!

1. Fill out your clear Personal, & Professional goals for the week.
2. Write an inspiring message to yourself.
3. Fill in the week.
4. Create an Action Task specifically for each of the 10 Alignments for the week.
5. At the end of each day, mark an X for each of the Action Tasks you completed.
6. Tally up your X's for that day, 1-10, and write in the bottom box.
7. At the end of the week, add up your daily totals and put a weekly total score out of 7.
8. Keep track of your cumulative weekly scores where you rank in each of the 10 Alignments.
9. Prioritize change and focus accordingly. Happy Hustle in each Alignment!

Here's a filled-out version of the Blissful Balancer as an example.

HAPPY ☺ HUSTLE™
BLISSFUL BALANCER
BALANCE = HAPPINESS

WEEK OF: September 20th-26th

PERSONAL GOAL OF THE WEEK Do at least one random act of kindness everyday.
PROFESSIONAL GOAL OF THE WEEK Make over 10k in net revenue!
THIS WEEK'S MESSAGE TO MYSELF Be present and grateful every moment, you never know when it could be your last.

10 ALIGNMENTS	ACTION TASK	M	T	W	T	F	S	S	SCORE
SELFLESS SERVICE	Give 15 minutes of time/expertise to someone in need	X	X		X	X		X	5
OPTIMIZED HEALTH	Exercise for 25 minutes and drink 1 gallon of water	X		X	X	X	X		5
UNPLUG DIGITALLY	Don't touch devices for the first 30 mins after waking up		X	X		X		X	4
LOVING RELATIONSHIPS	Send a gratitude text to one person you care about	X	X	X	X		X	X	6
MINDFUL SPIRITUALITY	Meditate for 10 minutes, focusing on your breath and gratitude				X	X		X	3
ABUNDANCE FINANCIALLY	Send email to one new perspective client/partnership opportunity	X	X	X	X	X	X	X	7!
PERSONAL DEVELOPMENT	Read inspirational and educational book for 20 minutes	X	X		X	X	X	X	6
PASSIONATE HOBBIES	Participate in 1 fun activity that brings you joy		X	X	X	X		X	5
IMPACTFUL WORK	Post 1 inspiring social media content sharing your message	X	X		X	X	X	X	5
NATURE CONNECTION	Go for a walk outside without your device for 15 minutes	X	X	X	X		X	X	6

Add up daily X's for total weekly Alignment score. Prioritize change accordingly. Score rubric: 7!=Ultimate Happy Hustler, 6=Happy Hustler, 5=A, 4=B, 3=C, 2=D, 1=F

"HAPPY HUSTLE YOUR DREAM REALITY AND LIVE A LIFE OF PASSION, PURPOSE, & POSITIVE IMPACT!"
WWW.THEHAPPYHUSTLE.COM

Blissful Balancer Alignment Weekly Score Rubric:

1 = **F**
2 = **D**
3 = **C**
4 = **B**
5 = **A**
6 = **Happy Hustler**
7! = **Ultimate Happy Hustler**

Author's Note: This rubric is different from the 10 Alignments Score Rubric because we made this purposefully for the Blissful Balancer which tracks binary daily action tasks completion accumulated for the week.

AGAIN, WHAT YOU MEASURE YOU CAN MANAGE! Keep track of your scores and watch yourself transform into a Happy Hustler! Now it's time to really get into the juicy goodness of the Happy Hustle, I'm talking about the 10 Alignments. We're kicking things off with Selfless Service, one of my personal favorites so keep on keepin' on!

ALIGNMENT 1
SELFLESS SERVICE

"THE SECRET TO LIVING IS GIVING."
TONY ROBBINS

Achieve Ultimate Fulfillment: Live With Selfless Service & Give Abundantly

By now you know, living a life of passion, purpose, and a positive impact is what the Happy Hustle is all about. The positive impact you have on others and the world, is ultimately what creates true bliss, that feeling of fulfillment. The peace you seek in your heart and certainty in your soul is knowing that you lived for more than just your personal aspirations.

The service over self-mindset is one of the greatest gifts I could ever dream to awaken within you. If you read this book and are left with nothing else but this newfound knowledge, I would consider the 2 ½ years writing this bad boy completely worth every painstaking minute. For the ripple effect of you spreading your joy, touches not just those you serve but far beyond.

And with enough people on board the service over self express train to transcendence, we can balance and harmonize the world while raising the collective vibration. Love is the way, and service is GPS.

Let service guide you to a higher purpose. An empathetic, enlightened existence. Start today, in just a small way. Just start.

Fulfillment Comes With Service

You may be thinking, "But Cary, I can barely pay my rent/mortgage let alone give anything to others." Well, I am going to outline some of the ways I practiced my service over self mindset (before I had money to give) and how you can too. I promise you: The service over self mindset paradoxically adds just as much (if not more) value to yourself as it does to those you are serving. The feeling of living this way is the true essence of why we are all here: to help one another; to serve.

Give Time

Arguably the most valuable commodity you could ever give is your time. You cannot replenish time like you can money, therefore the value is incomparable. If you have more time than money right now, find a cause that speaks to your soul and donate your time. Sign up to be a Big Brother or Sister, feed the homeless, work at an animal Rescue, discover, and decide where you wish to serve. Note: This time may not always be "easy" or "fun" as you experience difficult elements in the service of your cause. Persevere anyway.

After playing soccer with these awesome kids in one of the poorest slums in Cartagena, Columbia, Steph and I donated both time & money to help further their education.

Give $

If you have your basic needs met, a roof over your head, food in the fridge, and clothes on your back, chances are you can allocate funds to give something to others in need. If you aren't willing to give 10 cents out of a dollar, you aren't going to give 100,000 out of a million. I know, I know, "But Cary, when I have a million dollars, I will for sure give to others in need, just right now money is a little tight."

The time is now. Don't wait to give. Live in abundance and know that the universe will always manifest more. Find a cause that you can donate to today and give 10% of your last paycheck.

Give Expertise

Let's say that you want to take it a step further and not just give time or money, but you want to enrich the lives of those you are called to serve with knowledge. Sharing your expertise with those you are serving has the potential to be the most rewarding of all. By giving your expertise, you can change the trajectory of one's life indefinitely. There's an old proverb that states, "Give a man a fish, you feed him for a day. Teach a man to fish, you feed him for a lifetime." Who can you teach to fish? Whatever fishing is for you, mentor those in need and bless your life with fulfillment.

Steph & I supporting our troops by giving expertise and sharing the Happy Hustle message to a group of soldiers while on a US Military Base in South Carolina.

Schedule Giving

The best way to ensure you give regularly is to schedule it. You can schedule weekly visits, regular mentorship phone or video calls, the point is to create acts of service that get scheduled. I've found that creating calendar reminders that prompt me to donate my time, money or expertise is extremely effective. You can also take it a step further and schedule automatic payments to be routed from your account to organizations you wish to serve.

I like to use KIVA for this. You can provide loans/donations directly to social and environmental entrepreneurs in 3rd world countries and impoverished areas. The best part is 100% of your money goes directly to the person you are supporting and it's all automated so it takes from your account each month. Make giving a priority and schedule it. You will find happiness in the hustle when giving is present, guaranteed.

Accountability Through Community

Another way to ensure you are actively practicing the service over self mindset is by creating accountability through your community organization or with those directly in which you serve. Let's say you join the Big Brother and Big Sisters organization and you forget to pick up your little brother/sister on your scheduled day, then you will most likely feel like shit and surely not want to disappoint in the future. Accountability is essential in all areas. :)

HAPPY HUSTLER SPOTLIGHT

Leila Janah

Born to Indian immigrant parents, the inspiring social entrepreneur, Leila Janah was driven by the belief that "Talent is equally distributed, but opportunity is not."

She founded Samasource in Kenya with the mission to improve the lives of those living below the poverty line. The company has helped more than 50,000 people lift themselves out of poverty and has become one of the largest employers in East Africa.

Besides Samasource, Janah was the founder and CEO of LXMI, a fair-trade, organic skincare company, and Samaschool, a non-profit organization that trains people in digital skills. Leila spearheaded a global impact sourcing movement and was a champion for environmental sustainability and ending global poverty.

She also wrote a powerful book called Give Work: Reversing Poverty One Job at a Time -- which is worth the read.

Beautiful both inside and out, sadly at the young age of 37, due to complications from epithelioid sarcoma, a rare soft-tissue cancer, she died on January 24th, 2020. Her commitment to creating a better world was unparalleled. The ripple effects of her work will be felt for generations to come.

STORY TIME: 52K IN MISSING MONEY?!
THE GUATEMALAN GIVEBACK

I want to share with you a story of selflessly giving. Stay with me as I give you a bit of context. In 2016, my brother Grant went on vacation to rural Guatemala and visited a small Mayan village on beautiful Lake Atitlan where our mom was living (remember she's an old hippie by nature and loves to travel). He instantly fell in love with the people and culture, as did my mom. Many of the indigenous locals live on less than $1 a day, have very little access to education or opportunity, and 7 out of 10 children suffer the effects of chronic malnutrition. He came across a local non-profit community center that provides lunch every weekday to the most at-risk individuals to strengthen and stabilize the weakest members of this impoverished community. After speaking with the founders and directors, he learned that they were in desperate need of help. My brother agreed to join the team as a business consultant, brought on my sister Megan as a nonprofit consultant, Steph as a brand and communications specialist, and I joined to help with all of the marketing and implementation.

Grant put his business school skills to the test and did a deep audit on the business. Collecting and analyzing all the data points of their organization, which were basically hand-written notes in three different languages (Spanish, English, and Katchiquel-their local dialect) without any clear organization, filing, or accounting systems. He quickly realized how in shambles they were. After crunching the numbers, he identified over $52,000 dollars in missing donation money! He knew something was fishy about one of the American women executives in charge of the financials but never expected this. Knowing that these poor children live on literally less than a dollar a day, and how far that missing money could go, and that his greedy woman was laundering the donations into a private account to apparently buy local property was sickening. Following some serious detective work and with extreme tactfulness, Megan and Grant approached the non-profit board members and director with the proof of the missing money and who had taken it. They were all shocked. Talk about a lack of integrity.

They approached the woman with a lawsuit ordering the money to be returned. She knew she was caught and so did her lawyer father. In lieu of charges, he covered her by rightfully returning every penny. She was then ousted from the organization. It was now time to rebuild the non-profit.

Rebuild the non-profit is exactly what we did. Steph, Megan, Grant, my mom, and myself all donated time, money and expertise to help the cause. We organized a massive fundraiser locally, hosted a community event, redesigned their website and logo, created captivating content, participated in new and improved programs with the kids, and so much more. This experience positively impacted my life in so many ways and I still can recall the pure joy attained from my time spent on the ground in Guatemala giving to those in need. So, my Happy Hustlin' friend, find a way to give today and adopt the selfless service mindset. I'm telling ya, you will be so grateful you did. As Tony Robbins says, "Success without fulfillment is the ultimate failure." And one of the fastest paths to fulfillment is to help others.

ACTIONABLE TAKEAWAY

One of the fastest paths to fulfillment is to help others. Give that time, money, and/or expertise, and skyrocket your happiness!

EMBARRASSING FUN FACT

I have been court-mandated to volunteer 2 times in my life. Once, for being a bad boy (enough said) and once for speeding on my motorcycle after getting pulled over going 178 mph which resulted in a very large fine and 100 community service hours. And now instead, I volunteer by choice. ;)

POWERFUL RESOURCES

Book:
Building Social Business by Muhammed Yunnus
Give Work: Reversing Poverty One Job at a Time by Leila Janah

Podcast:
Giving Back Podcast

Movie:
Schindler's List

ALIGNMENT 2
OPTIMIZED HEALTH

"TAKE CARE OF YOUR BODY, IT'S THE ONLY PLACE YOU HAVE TO LIVE." – JIM ROHN

Happy Hustlin' Health: The Foundation of a Happy Life is a Healthy Life

This isn't a "health book" per se, however, optimizing your health is essential for success in every area of your life. When you are sick, almost everything else takes a back seat. That is why focusing proactively on embodying a healthy lifestyle is imperative to Happy Hustlin' your dream reality. You've heard the saying: "You are what you eat." Well, it's freaking true in many regards. I cannot stress enough the importance of eating healthy, organic fruits, vegetables, and whole foods.

Regardless of where you measured yourself on Da Assessment, 1-5 in the Optimized Health Alignment, we can all agree on the importance of consistently improving your health. Literally, if you could only do one thing right now to optimize your health for the rest of your life, I would say making the shift to a whole food, natural diet is going to have the greatest impact. Yes, that means cutting out the processed crap. No more sodas, sugar candies, junk food, etc. If you can't pronounce every ingredient on the label, don't eat it!

Now you're probably saying, "Geese, Cary no Oreo's or Coca Cola is a real buzz kill bro. That sounds extreme."

Listen, I'm all for sweets, and I'm not saying you can't have them every once in a while, but just choose to make it natural sweets. You can use naturally sweet apples to make an organic apple cobbler. You can make coconut milk ice cream with natural cacao nibs. You can eat papaya and watermelon with nothing but a spoon.

The point is, if you want to be a Happy Hustler, find ways to be extremely diligent as to what you put in your body. Every single bite has an effect either positively or negatively, whether you notice it or not. I recommend not getting caught up with the fad diet, but rather focusing that attention on simply eating, juicing, and blending an all-whole food organic diet. Of course, indulge in the occasional natural sweets. My guilty pleasure is fruit-filled muffins of all types, but I don't discriminate. Point being, food is thy medicine so be diligent with your diet.

Another highly debated topic is the perfect exercise routine. Look, I'm not going to overcomplicate it. Whether you want to do CrossFit, hot yoga, HIIT workouts, strength training, you name it, the most important aspect of exercise is just doing something consistently. I recommend moving the body at least 25-45 minutes every single day in some way. The goal should be to sweat and increase your strength, flexibility, and functional movement. Elevating your heart rate in each of your workouts to the point where you need to breathe out of your mouth and not just your nose is also beneficial. Doing this trains your body to move oxygen and blood to your muscles more efficiently and effectively.

Coupling this breathing with diversification is the key to my uber simple training philosophy. I make sure to switch it up and confuse my muscles and body with various exercises to avoid plateaus and stagnation while maintaining my size and strength. You can often find me doing bodyweight exercises like handstands, planks, push-ups, and pull-ups as those are the cornerstones of my routine. I then like to layer in kettlebell work, steel mace flow, TRX bands, punching and kicking (both on a heavy bag and shadow boxing), and groundwork (like bear crawls and animal movements) to keep it interesting.

The key to it all is consistency and doing something every day. Speaking of which, all this talk of exercising has got me craving a sweat. Be back soon, got to go get it in!

Side note: If you spend more time watching other people sweat (ie: sports on TV) vs sweating yourself, that's usually a good indicator that you need to level up your exercise and get your ass in the game.

Ok, you knew I'd have to mention health if I'm talking about happiness. Because we are nothing without our health. It is something I take very seriously. The term biohacking has become all the rage lately. To me, biohacking is an uncommon strategy to optimize your daily performance and fight fat, fatigue, and chronic illnesses. It's the act of utilizing ancient wisdom and modern science.

In reality, my mom was and is an OG Biohacker. She is a chiropractor by trade but has earned a functional medicine degree as well as training from both Eastern and Western medical schools of thought. She raised us with healthy, organic foods and a holistic lifestyle. I distinctly remember always having herbal teas instead of sodas and vegetable snacks instead of junk food. We rarely, if ever, took antibiotics and she fought to avoid vaccinations. I have never been vaccinated (WHOA, mic drop) and am still living, breathing, and thriving. We would heal ourselves naturally and use herbal and plant medicines to combat illness.

I have since studied holistic remedies, researched functional medicine, tested the latest alternative medicines, and little by little, ultimately biohacked myself to optimal wellness. Since then, I have joined forces with a premier biohacking company and have replicated the process of mixing ancient wisdom and modern science, helping thousands of clients all over the world regain and optimize their health using our proprietary system.

So, I am going to share with you some of my favorite biohacks for Happy Hustlin' your health based on the holistic biohacking mentality I have forged. For the record, unless it's an emergency, I do not take traditional medication, antibiotics, or any other pharmaceutical drug. Even when I had my ACL, ankle, and 2 nose surgeries (I've had a deviated septum from breaking my nose fighting & surfing... #growingpains), I didn't even take the pain meds. I believe in the holistic approach to health care whenever possible.

The goal is to share with you what I do and hopefully provide a couple of actionable takeaways that you can apply to your life and health right away.

Biohacking 101

Naked Push & Pull

We're going to start simple. One of the things that I am religious about and have been doing for as long as I can remember is doing push-ups, pull-ups (if there's a pull-up bar nearby), and sit-ups before every shower. Yes, that means I usually end up doing them naked. I do push-ups until it hurts. Not necessarily to max out, but just enough to feel the burn, and then do 10 more. These bodyweight exercises are timeless and you can do them virtually anywhere. Whether you are traveling and in a hotel room or staying at a friend's house, if there's a floor, you can do push-ups and sit-ups. So no excuses! Let's start a #nakedpushups movement, y'all.

Ice Baths

Two of my favorite ways to Happy Hustle my health are with cold and hot thermogenesis. That is a fancy way of saying ice baths and infrared saunas. The benefits of the ice baths are vast. Not only does hopping in a pool of ice cold 40 degree water, usually ranging between 38-48 degrees, for 3 minutes mentally strengthen your mind, but it will increase the blood flow throughout your cardiovascular system. Also, ice baths decrease inflammation and burn calories as your body naturally will attempt to heat itself up. I recommend, at the minimum, taking a cold shower once a day or at least finishing each shower with 30 seconds of cold. In life, we have to do things we don't want to do. Each time I force myself to take an ice bath or cold shower, I am training my brain to do things I don't feel like doing but know that I need to, a.k.a. creating discipline and mental fortitude.

Remember: *Discipline = Freedom.*

Saunas

Infrared or dry saunas are an amazing Happy Hustle Hack to detox your body and lose weight. Raising your core body temperature induces an artificial fever. How does this benefit the body? Well, fever is the body's natural mechanism to strengthen and accelerate the immune response. This enhances the immune system and when combined with the improved elimination of toxins and wastes via intense sweating, you'll increase your overall health and resistance to disease.

By sitting on your bum in a sauna, you are literally sweating out the toxins and increasing your metabolism in the process. Using a sauna can also decrease stress and increase muscle recovery. Increased blood circulation carries off metabolic waste products and delivers oxygen-rich blood to oxygen-depleted muscles, so they recover faster.

Product Recommendation:

One of my favorite biohack's is my full-spectrum infrared sauna: Therasage Thera360 Plus.
You can get the hook up when you use code: "HAPPY" on everything at **www.therasage.com**
Plus it's a family-owned company that actually cares about their customers!

Soakin' up some full-spectrum infrared red light in my Thera360 Plus Sauna.

Sunlight and Stretch

Every morning when you wake up, one of the best things you can do to kickstart your day is to get direct sunlight and stretch your body. Sunlight is the source of life's energy. When natural sunlight is absorbed through your skin, it triggers the body's production of Vitamin D. Vitamin D is a crucial ingredient for your overall health and helps protect against inflammation, lowers blood pressure, helps muscle recovery, and improves brain function - not to mention that it may even protect against cancer. If needed, you can also supplement with Vitamin D + K2. Disclaimer: *Consult with your doctor before taking anything.*

However, the key is not to burn the skin as burning has an adverse effect on your health. Natural sunlight can improve vision and repair your eyes. I sun gaze every morning for a couple of minutes in the downward dog position looking back and up through my legs about 45 degrees off the sun (not directly at it).

I then stretch usually shirtless in the sun. It is said that stretching every day can add 7 years to your life. Stretching allows blood and nutrients to flow throughout your body which reduces soreness and increases recovery. Stretching also helps prevent injuries and will improve your range of motion. So, get out there and touch your toes, baby! Even better if you stretch in the sun y'all. It is no brainer to charge up your body in the morning.

And if you're feeling especially froggy, throw some shadow boxing kicks and punches in there, do a little Tai Chi, or jam your favorite tune and bust out an ecstatic dance. All these things will help your body and also elevate your mood. After all, we are Happy Hustlin' out here so might as well have some fun!

Supplementation

Here's my take on supplements: less is more. If you can get the nutrients from whole foods, veggies, and fruits -- do it. If you can't and need to supplement, be diligent with which supplements you use. Many supplements are crap and just an isolated form of the real deal. Read the labels and reviews before purchasing or consuming.

With that being said, there is one company that I use their supplements religiously and that is Bioptimizers. They make a powerful probiotic called P3-OM, a digestive enzyme called MassZyme and properly formulated magnesium formula that is a gamechanger for enhancing sleep called Magnesium Breakthrough.

Most people are deficient in magnesium. Magnesium Breakthrough is my go-to.

These 3 are a staple in my routine.
You can check them out at **www.bioptimizers.com**
and use **code: HAPPY** to save you some moolah.

Do your research and ask an expert if you're unsure about supplements. It is also extremely beneficial to get annual blood tests. Some of the supplements that your ripped healthy friend recommended may work great for them but you have a completely different cellular DNA makeup - thus the importance of testing and not guessing. When you know your lab results, which include your vitamin and mineral deficiencies, the environmental and genetic mismatches, and the toxins that may be hindering your performance, then you can make educated decisions based on what you actually need.

Many people take too many supplements that often end up as expensive urine or actually causing complications. Don't be that person. I take only the supplements I feel are necessary that I cannot otherwise get from food, and when I do take them, they are scientifically validated, 3rd party tested, and are based on my blood work needs. Point is, everything you put in your body has an effect. Be diligent.

HAPPY HUSTLER SPOTLIGHT

Danette May

I had the privilege of getting to know Danette May at a mastermind in Utah back in 2018. Her kind energy lit up the room and we shared many of the same core values regarding health and nutrition as well as our common upbringing in Montana.

She is definitely a Happy Hustler and is also America's leading healthy lifestyle expert, #1 best-selling author of The Rise along with 7 health and fitness books and programs. And she is the co-founder and CCO of Mindful Health, LLC (#48 on the Inc. 5000 List), Earth Echo Foods, a dedicated founder of The Rise movement, a world-renowned motivational speaker, a wife, and a mother.

In addition to being named #16 on Women's Fitness list of fitness & health leaders for 2018, Danette has recently been featured in the culture-shifting documentary, WeRiseUP, alongside His Holiness the Dalai Lama, Alanis Morissette, Lance Bass, Amina Mohammed, Marie Forleo, Richard Branson, Barbara Marx Hubbard, Julia Ormond, and many other high-impact, accomplished leaders.

Since 2011, she's helped transform the physical, mental, emotional, and spiritual lives of millions of people around the world by focusing on healing foods, healing movement, and a healing mind. Her impactful mission is simple, yet profound! She and I both believe in the holistic approach to health and wellness. She inspires people to dig deep into their souls to find out who they really are, to construct the life of their dreams, and stand fully in their power. Danette and I would both agree, whatever you want in this life, it is all possible, but not without taking care of and optimizing your health!

STORY TIME: MY SOCCER CAREER AND THE INJURY THAT CHANGED THE PLANS...

Balance is the key to unlocking the optimal health that you desire. Balance in your workouts, balance in your recovery, balance in your diet. For instance, if I work out super hard in the gym, have a soccer game, and train Krav Maga all in the same day, I know that I will need to prioritize my recovery and potentially reduce the intensity over the next two days. Balancing recovery with performance is essential. I will also need to make sure to fuel my recovery with nourishing whole foods.

When it comes to health, I got to be honest with ya, I take it pretty seriously. I made a commitment to myself when I was a boy to always stay healthy & be a ninja (more on this later) both mentally and physically. I know that health is the cornerstone of Happy Hustlin' my dream reality. The question is: Do you accomplish the little things and hold yourself accountable? Meaning if you say you're going to work out, hold yourself accountable and work out. If you say you're going to eat healthy, well hold yourself accountable and eat healthy. The best abs are made in the kitchen. You can do crunches until you are blue in the face, but if you're going to slam a frozen pizza after every workout, you will never get abs or optimal health.

I learned the principles of doing the little things and holding myself accountable at an early age as a competitive athlete. My whole life was focused on high performance. I know that if I want to excel in the field, I must prioritize my health and wellness off the field. If I don't sleep well, I know my performance the next day would be negatively affected. If I don't eat right and stuff my face with garbage junk food, I know the next day that my performance would be sluggish and "off". If I didn't work out consistently and skipped days, I know my momentum would be shot and come game time, my performance would suffer. In order to Happy Hustle your dream reality, optimal health is imperative.

I want to share with you a little bit of my journey as a soccer player as it relates to optimizing health. Soccer is and has been my passion. It was my dream to play professionally. I even went as far as training to play for the Olympic Development Program as a US National Team hopeful. I started playing at the age of 3 and instantly gravitated to the sport's non-stop action and intensity. I was never the best player on the field, but I was always the hardest worker. At an early age, older teams would recruit me to play with them even though I was years younger. I planned my life around soccer. I played other sports like basketball (which I got MVP of my middle school season without even scoring one point—all due to hard work #beastpracticeplayer), football in high school (admittedly, just so I could wear the jersey on Fridays to school and date the head cheerleader), and baseball throughout my childhood (which was my second favorite and I was pretty decent at. Many of my past teammates are playing in the Big's these days -- but soccer was my go-to. I had to choose a sport to focus on in high school, so I naturally chose soccer.

I was playing for a high-level club travel team in which we competed in all of the state and national competitions. I was positioning myself for a Division-1 scholarship and my goal was to get a full ride. I spent hours upon hours practicing, watching film, and submitting to scouts. When it came to my senior year of high school, expectations were indeed high, especially since our team won the state conference the year prior and became the team to beat, returning the majority of our starting 11.

It was our first home game of the season. I was the captain of the team and starting center-midfielder, and I was ready to give my all. With college scouts in the stands, it was GO time. The whistle blew. It couldn't have been more than 15 minutes into my first game as a senior when the heartbreak took place. I was attempting to block a clearance from one of their defenders with my left foot. As I lunged to block the ball, the defender kicked the ball and followed through into my foot, sharply inverting (towards my other leg) my unplanted ankle. I (and the players around me) heard an ear-piercing pop. I screamed in pain and instantly dropped to the ground holding my ankle. I tried to get back up as soon as possible but couldn't. Unlike many of the other soccer players who give the rest of us a bad rap, I was not a player who faked injuries for foul calls. My teammates helped me over to the sidelines, and I knew it was no bueno. It immediately swelled up to the size of a grapefruit, and I couldn't put any weight on it.

I went to my mom's chiropractic office for x-rays and an ultrasound assessment after the game ended. I'm very grateful that she had the equipment and knowledge because injuries were common in our family. Going hard often equates to getting hurt. The x-rays revealed I had broken my ankle. Later, an MRI revealed that I also had torn two major ligaments. My season was over. My previous verbal D1 college scholarship offers were swept out from under me. Often teams do not invest in a player with ankle or

knee injuries as they are typically recurring. The reality began to sink in at the doctor's office. My life as a soccer player and my dream of becoming a professional player didn't seem promising...
or so I thought.

I didn't get any offers to the D1 schools I planned on playing for (USF, UCF, North Carolina). I didn't get many offers at all. Only a couple of teams had seen me play before my injury and, when I graduated from high school, my choices were Montana State University, Elmhurst College in Chicago, and Florida Gulf Coast. Ultimately, I was still able to solidify a scholarship and enjoyed 3 years as an NCAA collegiate player but it never was at the level I previously imagined. I went on to live and study abroad in Barcelona, Spain during my 4th and senior year but that ankle injury indeed changed the trajectory of my life.

Back when my quads were on point. Ahh the glory days.

In Spain, I would dribble the streets and play pick-up games daily with the locals. I stumbled upon a 4th division professional team practicing in the barrio of Le Champla one night when I was out dribbling and began watching through the fence. After practice, I went up to the coach with my broken Spanish/Catalan (the local language in Barca) and asked if I could try out. The next week, the coach gave me a shot. It was A team vs. B team scrimmage day. This gringo didn't get into the game until the 80th minute after the A team scored yet another goal which meant that the B team (aka my team) was now losing 3-1. They put me at center back, and from the kick-off, the ball was passed back to me. I took one touch to my right and, I shit you not, proceeded to hit the best ball of my life to the left forward streaking down the side of the field towards goal. I mean this ball knuckled and floated in a perfect line as if Messi himself had passed it. The left forward chest-trapped the ball and volleyed the ball first-time past the goalie and into the back of the net. Everyone looked at me like wtf, who's this guy?' I looked at my right foot like wtf, where'd that come from?

I ended up making the team, playing around Barca for a bit, and getting paid a small salary per game. I could barely understand the pre-game or halftime speeches as they were in Catalan (thank goodness for my Italian teammate/translator). I wouldn't say by any means that I fulfilled my dream of playing pro, but I did get paid to play, and that was cool, and I'm very grateful for that time in my life, even though my ankle injury plagued my career and was constantly an issue. I still have to wear braces and wrap my ankles every time I play, but at least I can compete on Sundays in Men's League (where I still GO HARD ;). My biggest takeaway:

"Life doesn't always turn out how you intend. Plans change. Things happen. But your health will always remain a priority."

I thought I was destined for soccer player greatness. I was physically and mentally able, but one injury can change it all. Just like in life, one bad decision can change it all. In business, in sports, in relationships, sometimes we have clear plans but it just doesn't turn out that way for whatever reason. Regardless if I'm playing professional sports or not, I know that my health is essential to my happiness and to my life's success. And it is for you too. You must make sure that you really do the little things and hold yourself accountable every day. Focus on your routine both in the morning and in the evening. Watch what you consume and cut out the garbage foods. In order to be a true Happy Hustler, do not slack in this area.

ACTIONABLE TAKEAWAY

You can have everything you want in this life and more, but in order to get it, you must have the energy to work for it. Your energy is directly correlated with your cellular health. And your cellular health is directly correlated to your daily habits. If you want to perform at the highest level in your particular field, then you have to exercise and eat healthy. You have to balance intense workouts with intense recovery. This chapter on optimizing your health is pivotal to your performance. Go back through and actually implement what you've learned into your routine. I hope I've made my point in this chapter in regard to just how freaking significant your health truly is to your overall success and happiness. Do the little things, hold yourself accountable, and optimize that health, baby!

EMBARRASSING FUN FACT

I once competed in a push-up contest on MTV's stage at Panama City Beach with a chick in a bikini sitting on my back. I know, douche alert. It was a different time back then, gimme a break… and for the record, I got second.

POWERFUL RESOURCES

Books:
How to Eat, Live, and Be Healthy by Paul Chek
Own The Day by Aubrey Marcus
Headstrong & Gamechangers by Dave Asprey

Podcasts:
Ben Greenfield Podcast
The Model Health Show with Sean Stevenson

Movie:
The Gamechanger

ALIGNMENT 3
UNPLUG DIGITALLY

"DISCONNECTING FROM OUR TECHNOLOGY TO RECONNECT WITH OURSELVES IS ABSOLUTELY ESSENTIAL FOR WISDOM." ARIANNA HUFFINGTON

Put The Phone Down For A Digital Detox

One of the biggest things holding you back from viscerally connecting with yourself, others, and nature is that little rectangle made of plastic & glass in your pocket. Yes, I'm poorly describing your cell phone. That fuckin' thing is what I like to call a time sucker.

It will suck all the time you want to give it and never give that time back, all of which can be used elsewhere, for things like being in nature, connecting with the natural world, and tapping into your soul. One of the best things I usually do in my week is a digital detox on Sundays. I refrain from using any phone/computer/tablet/tv or other tech. I'll put all of my devices in a closet or drawer, completely out of sight, and not touch them until 24 hours have passed from the time that they went in. I make time to get outside and tap into my true self. I am still, present, and at peace. I highly recommend this for you too.

We often don't realize just how inundated we are by the constant notifications, calls, emails, texts, alerts, news, social media dopamine dumps, and unconscious societal pressures that plague our every waking moment. It's like we are constantly "on". Even the strongest computers in the world need to power down and do a reset from time to time… and so do you.

But when you do a digital detox, you can find the freedom and fulfillment that you so eagerly seek is already present within you. You don't have to go far. Just put the phone down, get outside, and enjoy what really matters.

EMFs And Dopamine

Since we're talking about unplugging digitally, we have to talk about the EMFs our devices emit and the dopamine dumpin' that comes from using them. Electromagnetic Fields (EMFs) are all around us and they are affecting our health. Especially now with 5G. Our smartphones, computers, Wi-Fi routers, smart TVs, tablets, smartwatches, wireless headphones, microwaves, electric cars, etc., all emit EMFs.

Essentially, anything that can connect to the internet could be negatively affecting your health. To mitigate your risk and exposure, you must be deliberate with how you use these items. I recommend at the minimum unplugging your Wi-Fi at night, turning all of your devices on airplane mode when not using them, and spending time each day digitally detoxing. As mentioned above, I like to spend all of Sunday usually doing a digital detox where I completely unplug. Now, this is often easier said than done, but boy is it refreshing to come back on Monday after 24 hours of tech liberation. Give it a shot and let me know how great you feel afterwards.

It's important to mention the effects of tech, and especially social media, on your brain. See, every time you get a notification your brain sends a chemical messenger called dopamine along a reward pathway that makes you feel good. Dopamine is associated with activities like sex, food, exercise, love, gambling, and now, social media. The problem is that when your brain releases dopamine due to social media, it is weakening your brain's ability to concentrate and simultaneously causing you to become addicted to the "dopamine rush". Thus then making you want to check your phone constantly. Point is, resist the urge and unplug. *Use tech wisely, don't let it use you!*

Set Barriers

If you really want to become the master of your devices, then you must set barriers and actually stick to them! For example, a barrier for me is I do not touch my devices 60 minutes after waking up and 60 minutes before going to bed. This gives my mind, body, and soul time to be present without the distractions of technology during two of the most important parts of the day. Try doing this and watch your happiness increase. Even if you just start with 30 minutes in the morning and 30 minutes in the evening, you will notice a difference.

HAPPY HUSTLER SPOTLIGHT

Cowboy Duncan Vezain

Now when it comes to being unplugged digitally, I gotta say it is hard to find a role model in this Alignment, since it seems we are so plugged in all the time. But, if there was one for me, it would be my good buddy one-eyed Cowboy Duncan. This guy is the toughest, most legit cowboy I know.

He lives his life outdoors, working with horses and his hands. He was born and raised in Montana and spends his time ranching, roping, riding bulls, competing in rodeos, building saddles, making leather items, shoeing horses, building wagons, breaking horses, branding cattle, recording a music album, shooting movies, slangin' side-shooters, crackin' whips, you name it. Anything western this guy has done it! He works a lot with Hollywood movies and tv shows that are shot out west as the go-to horse wrangler and often as the talent. Usually for the bad guy - due to his eye patch, it's a natural-looking role for him ;). But that's not why I featured him in this Happy Hustler spotlight.

He is unplugged digitally during the majority of his days. Despite being disconnected, he is reachable, and will always call you back, and do what he says he'll do. If he says he will be at the trailhead at 7:00 AM with five horses ready to ride, then by golly he'll be there. He has a website for his business. He has a phone number. And that's about it. No social media. No other bs. He makes hand-shake deals and is a man of his word. He's a family man with a beautiful wife and 2 amazingly independent daughters. He lives a simple, hard-working, successful Happy Hustlin' life. He is an example of what is possible if you want to master a craft (or multiple) instead of playing the social media online guru game. He has positioned himself as THE guy for his skills in his area and people reach out to him, as opposed to him marketing to them. I've seen first-hand this rewarding way of life and I must say, oftentimes I am envious of the sheer simplicity. So, see if you can simplify your life by unplugging more from your devices, quiet all the noise that comes with them, and get back to what's important.

Dunc & I on the annual Labor Day Montana Wagon Train… where we basically ride (and race) horses, drive wagons and camp out for 5 days… talk about some good ole' Western fun.

Steph & I swimming with Milo bareback in the "redneck water park" aka a muddy pond on one of the annual Labor Day Wagon Train's in Montana.

STORY TIME: MONTANA MASTERMIND EPIC CAMPING ADVENTURE

One of the ways that I truly love to unplug digitally is by going deep into the backcountry wilderness and disconnecting from technology completely. We host something every year, accurately called the Montana Mastermind Epic Camping Adventure. No phones, no laptops, no service. Completely off the grid. We disconnect to reconnect. We take high-level entrepreneurs hiking 10+ miles deep into the backcountry wilderness with backpacks filled with their personal gear. We pack horses in who carry the food and group camping gear, and set up basecamp around a pristine lake in a stunning canyon complete with 360-degree jaw-droppingly beautiful views.

There we spend 5 full days camping out while enjoying a structured itinerary. We learn primitive survival training (bow-drills, fire making, water purification, shelter building, hunting/gathering techniques, etc.) and master the art of fly fishing (everyone who attends gets their own fly rod/reel combo included). We do primal bodyweight workouts and natural cold plunges. We embark on powerful breathwork sessions and deep dive into lengthy medicinal mediations. And we sprinkle in structured business masterminds throughout in order to workshop our adversities and share what's working in our businesses. Plus, we're catered to by a professional backcountry chef who makes delicious and nutritious foods over a campfire. And we have a outdoor extraordinaire professional videographer and photographer capture all the epic footage!

This entire experience is absolutely rejuvenating. Most who've attended say it is "life-changing" and "an enlightening spiritual journey". See, we are rarely ever disconnected from our devices, and society for that matter, for more than a day, let alone five.

It's a helluva great time mixin' business and pleasure while digitally detoxing deep in the backcountry wilderness.

Most of the entrepreneurs who've attended said it was a "life-changing experience" and the digital detox was a complete reset that was "invaluable to their overall well-being".

The 2021 Montana Mastermind Epic Camping Adventure crew of rockstar Happy Hustlin' entrepreneurs!

There are so many highlights and powerful takeaways from these adventures...it's hard to name just a couple but here are **3 Actionable Takeaways.**

ACTIONABLE TAKEAWAYS

1. **Disconnect to reconnect**
Being without phones, laptops, tv's or devices allows us to tap into our primal, present, true selves. I recommend doing regular digital detoxes from this moment forward.

2. **Push your body and mind regularly**
We hiked roughly 20 miles round trip in the wilderness with a heavy pack on. We pushed ourselves physically with primal workouts, breathwork, hiking, fishing and more. We also pushed ourselves mentally by meditating, journaling, learning new primitive survival skills, fly fishing skills, and beyond. Pushing ourselves is how we grow our confidence and comfort zone.

3. **Surround yourself with a like-minded group of people who add value to your reality.**
As they say, you are the sum of your closest relationships. Being around other rock star entrepreneurs helped us mastermind our businesses and overcome personal adversity, and it will ultimately expedite our success. Also, be unapologetically yourself and laugh more (which we often did until our bellies hurt) while having fun with other like-minded people. This is what life is all about!

Not to mention, when you surround yourself with like-minded inspiring souls in such an environment, life-long bonds are forged. For those of you who are interested in attending, you can go to caryjack.com/montana and apply to see if it's a fit.

Regardless of whether you attend a Montana Mastermind Epic Camping Adventure or not, I recommend going off-grid for an extended period of time and tap into your primal self and un-distracted soul.

EMBARRASSING FUN FACT

I once lost my phone, wallet, and dignity while raging at a foam party in Ibiza, Spain. I didn't replace my phone for over a month and that was one of the absolute freest times in my life.

POWERFUL RESOURCES

Books:
Disconnect To Reconnect: How To Unplug And Get Your Life Back by Dr. Mike Steves

Podcasts:
The Happy Hustle Podcast – Episode #78, #164, #166

Movie:
The Social Dilemma

ALIGNMENT 4
LOVING RELATIONSHIPS

"WE ARE MOST ALIVE WHEN WE'RE IN LOVE." – JOHN UPDIKE

Listen, Add Value, Be Real

What is all this Happy Hustlin' for if you don't have love in your life? The ironic truth of human existence is that no matter how much shit we accomplish or money we make, it is ultimately other people that give these accomplishments meaning.

Every day your relationships are built up and torn down in the subtlest ways. It's the little things, day in and day out, that add up over time to unshakeable fulfillment or unsalvageable misery.

You decide how you treat the ones in your life that you care the most about. Do you take your significant other for granted? Do you push off your calls with your family members? Do you spend uninterrupted time with your kids or best friends or furry loved ones?

Realize that love needs energy to thrive. Sure, there will always be a special bond between a mother or father and their child. But this unconditional love, that most of us experience with our parents, often stops there.

The other relationships in our lives, ones with partners, husbands, wives, boyfriends, girlfriends, siblings, and best friends, need our energy, time, and attention to act in a manner that fosters a loving connection. If you stop giving these relationships your energy, they will eventually stop providing you with love.

Which relationships in your life are not being given enough energy, and therefore possibly lacking in love? I'm sure you can think of one, I know I can in my own life. Take stock right now.

Decide today to give that relationship energy by calling that person and connecting for at least 15 minutes today. Listen. Add value. Connect. Tell them you love them and that you are there for them. Happy Hustlers take action. Despite whatever rocky pasts, we can lead the way to a better future with all of our relationships through positive action and energy.

4 Things That Destroy Loving Relationships

It's important to note that there are 4 main contributing factors that actually destroy loving relationships in your life. Think about which of the following are currently present for you and how you can pivot accordingly.

Lack of Trust

Do you do what you say you're going to do? Because every time you don't, it adds a crack in the windshield of trust. Eventually it will shatter completely. Trust is errthang.

Disrespect Towards One Another

Do you treat your loved ones as you would want to be treated? Don't say anything in the heat of the moment today that will hurt tomorrow. Because you know them better than most, you can cut them deeper with hurtful words. Be kind and respectful even when shit hits the fan. I know that's easier said than done, more on this later.

Criticism or Judgment

Do you nitpick, criticize, and judge? Cut that shit out. Worry about yourself and not them. This is one I personally still work on. Don't just nitpick the bad, but rather see the good. If you focus on the problem, the problem expands. If you focus on the solution, the solution manifests.

Defensiveness and the Need to be Right

Do you often defend your point of view and feel the need to be right? Keep your EGO out of it, and when you're wrong, admit it. Would you rather make your point and be "right" or leave it lay and be happy? Sometimes, you have to surrender and just say sorry for the misunderstanding or miscommunication. Don't let petty problems fester as they are often not worth it. If you are doing any of these things in your relationships, cut the crap. Change your bad habits.

Everyone says there are plenty of fish in the sea. And I agree there are. Trust me, I used to be an avid fisherman. But that gets old. I am now in a loving relationship and have no interest in looking back. Of course, we have our shit and plenty of it. But usually when there are issues, I can trace it back to the lack of energy we are putting forth into our relationship or falling victim to one of the above-stated unhealthy habits.

When we get complacent and stop doing the coconut oil massages and making each other morning coffees, then tension arises. So keep putting in the energy and enjoy the love each and every day.

90 - 10 Ratio

I'm sure many of you have heard of Pareto's 80-20 law. Basically stating, 80% of your desired output is derived from 20% of your input. Well, in your relationship, I have a similar but different theory. I believe that if you are happy in your relationship 90% of the days in a month, then you should continue forward with your lover.

Now that leaves room for the occasional blow-up and drama, but it should only make up a small fraction of your time together.

Remember: "What you can measure, you can change and/or manage."

You can then assess how much love or struggle there is each week, each month, each year. It should ideally equate to 90% love days, with 10% room for those inevitable altercations.

Love Calendar

This is a tactic I've used in my relationship with great success. My partner and I call it the Love Calendar. Basically, you are creating your own internal rubric to assess your daily love number. I like to use a whiteboard calendar and hang it in our bedroom. Every evening, I ask my partner, "What was your love number today?" 10 would be tons of passion, joy, love, and sex.

1 would be the opposite, deep despair, arguments, no love or connection. If she says a 9 and you say a 7, then write the average (8) inside the heart for that day. If the score is 5 or over, it is a love day and you then draw a heart with the number inside of it on the calendar for that day. If the average of your two numbers is below a 5, then you write an X and the number in the calendar for that day. This gamification can make a huge positive impact on your loving relationship, as it does mine. It's helpful to see and quantify things in our lives. Hence, the creation of the 10 Alignments and weekly measurements.

Now, an important note: Keep the calendar in your bedroom and at the end of the month, assess how much love there was. If only 50% of the days were marked as love days that month, you guys got some work to do. It may even mean you want to reconsider the relationship entirely if this is a consistent theme month over month. If the calendar is 90% chock-full of hearts, awesome! You are in a healthy loving relationship and keep on keepin' on baby! :)

Love or Fear

It is said that every action stems from two basic emotions, either love or fear. When we are consciously aware, we can choose clearly. When we operate out of fear, we often are coming from a place of lack, angst, insecurity, or stress. Instead of giving into fear, choose to operate out of love in all of your relationships. I know, sounds woo-woo. But, hang in there.

Begin to recognize love and give it more freely. Allow love to be the reason behind what you do. Develop actions based on that feeling of goodness. Be caring, compassionate, and kind.

In your relationships and in your life, whenever you have an opportunity, share your kindness with others and witness the good karma of the universe circulate around you.

I'm advocating for the simple act of being kind with no alternative agenda. Hold the door open. Pick up a piece of litter. Carry someone's bag. These minor actions often derive from love. Each day, incorporate loving micro-tasks. Be that person who exudes kindness and leads with love, not fear.

Love Journal

Another tactic to foster more love in your partnership is to write down one thing you are grateful for in the other person every single day. My partner Steph and I use a journal specifically for daily gratitude and we each have a section where we write whatever comes to mind that we are grateful for that particular day about one another. You do not have to share it with them right away, or ever. But, you can if you'd like. By doing this, you'll start looking for new things to be grateful for as opposed to looking for things to nitpick.

At the end of each month, you can give each other your list to read and enjoy the love that follows. At the end of the day, relationships require constant effort. Like playing professional sports, you must practice every day in order to be the best you can be and to be able to crush it come game time to get the W. It's not enough to show up on game day or practice once a month.

You must put in the work and Happy Hustle for your relationship and "practice" every day. Love is effort multiplied. Every day, in every way, put in the constant effort to care, support, protect, respect, communicate, trust, and honor your significant other. Then, enjoy the results.

Love Yourself

It's time to love yourself (if you haven't lately ;). It seems like a dirty philosophical quest. But really, I just mean love and appreciate who you are. And if you don't currently feel that love for yourself, it's time to become who you want to love. You have to be able to wholeheartedly love yourself before you are able to love others. You may have heard this before, but it is so very true. Being at a place of inner peace attracts others into our lives that are in similar states. That is when unconditional love can manifest. That is when you inadvertently invite your soulmate into your life.

Full disclosure: I "played the field" (serial dated) like a savage in my early 20's. Sure, I enjoyed the chase and challenge. But, I was truly in a state of insecurity and searching for something I wasn't ready to find. Even when I was in a relationship, I was never fully able to commit and shed all of my layers.

Protecting myself in nearly every aspect, I was not in a place to entirely give to the individual, regardless of how great she was, for I had not yet fully given to myself. Being content with yourself will help to bring you the inner zen needed to attract and find a counterpart to share your journey with. Once I found myself in this place of peace, the universe provided me with exactly what I was searching for and more. And it will do the same for you.

When you start to live this way, you start to love yourself more. When you love yourself, you attract love from others. Without that self-love, finding a counterpart becomes an arduous endeavor. When we truly are at peace inside and love ourselves fully, we open ourselves up to love from others. We don't necessarily have to be content with our current career, situation, how much money we have in the bank, or where we are in life. But, we do need to accept the circumstances and love ourselves regardless. If we are genuinely seeking love, we must first search within.

We must practice self love. That is a part of Happy Hustlin'. Giving ourselves care and affection first and foremost. Similar to the experience on an airplane when the stewardess goes through their pre-flight routine. In case of an emergency, they instruct every passenger to put on their own oxygen mask, before assisting others. This is true for love and life. You are unable to help your loved ones nor the person next to you if you cannot breathe yourself. You have to love yourself first.

Once we are grounded, steadily breathing, and loving ourselves, we can then give from our overflow. We can give away the excess love and kindness that we possess. Our hearts are the strongest muscle in the body. So strong that it produces enough love to embrace everyone. The ability to furnish warmth is within us all. Whether with a first-time interaction or a long-time lover, we behold the incredible aptitude to love freely.

So, **choose self-love. Be kind to yourself.** Make strides to consciously be aware of your inner thoughts and your mind's chatter. Fill yourself with goodness, positive self-talk, and powerful affirmations. Then, you can share that love and kindness with others. Be open to receive the light. Be conscious of your choices, whether they are made from love or fear. Whenever possible, go out of your way to be nice. Implement love-oriented micro-tasks each day and notice the change in your world.

Life is about love. Give it, receive it, and actively be it.

A heart from me to you. :)

HAPPY HUSTLER SPOTLIGHT

Oprah

When I think of one of the world's greatest Happy Hustler's I think of Oprah. Not only is she a multi-billion-dollar media mogul, author, actress, and philanthropist, but she is kind and empathetic. She is humble. She is a hard worker. She truly cares about other people and has proven so time and time again with her generous acts of giving. Like the time she gave everyone in the audience of her hit talk show, The Oprah Winfrey Show (which ran for 25 years), a brand-new car.

She has been in a loving relationship with her partner Stedman since 1986. She overcame sexual abuse, gender inequality, and racism, amongst many other adversities on her ascension to becoming the global leader that she is today.

In 2013, Oprah was awarded the Presidential Medal of Freedom by President Obama and has received honorary doctorate degrees from Duke and Harvard. She is indeed a Happy Hustler and one who has made a massive impact on millions of lives all around the world... and fostering her loving relationships all the while.

STORY TIME: HOW WE MET....
SHE STOOD ME UP!

I feel that I would be remiss if I did not share this story in this book, so here we go. Let me preface this experience by reiterating that I have had plenty of fun and have "met" a lot of women from all over the world. But, never did I think I would fall so hard. It happens when you least expect it. It happens when you are at a place of true self-love. And it happens when you aren't necessarily looking or ready for it.

For me, in particular, it started one warm sunny afternoon in South Florida when I was booked for promo-modeling at The Breakers in Palm Beach. By promo-modeling I mean, paid to walk around a room full of wealthy women with a pair of high-end Manolo Blahniks (women's shoes) on a silver platter. In the midst of my route, I locked eyes with a tall, brown-eyed beauty in a gorgeous glitter gown. I shamelessly approached her with my platter in hand and sparked up a conversation. Her name was Stephanie and she was a film actress. We hit it off, both being from Florida, both involved in the entertainment industry, both loving nature and the great outdoors, and both promo-modeling at the same event. We exchanged social media profiles and that was that.

I continued my duties, as did she. The gig ended without much more than that initial exchange. Eight months went by and I had since moved to Bangkok, Thailand. I was modeling and acting, and it just so happens that same little Latina heat from Uruguay, Stephanie, commented on one of my modeling pictures from abroad. I had a pretty serious mustache and rattail at the time (as it is one of my favorite looks) while rocking a hipster, 3- piece suit get up. She commented, "Ok GQ, I see you over der. ;)".

The comment that started it all!

That was it. That was all I needed. I saw this comment from the other side of the world and couldn't get her out of my mind. I started lurking her profile nightly (#creeper) and I said to myself, "I'm for sure hitting her up when I get back."

So, I returned from my Southeast Asian adventures and immediately began to plant the seed. I sent her a FB message just catching up with some small talk. A little back and forth banter, if you will. Since it had been a while, and I barely knew her, building trust was essential. I then asked her to join me for a paddleboard and fishing evening excursion followed by biking beach cruisers to taco Tuesday... a pretty swell first date if I say so myself. She initially responded enthusiastically and the date was set. But apparently, there was a miscommunication in which we still both laugh and agree to disagree about the confirmation itself. Regardless, I proceeded to ready the paddle boards for this much-anticipated date. 5:00 PM (our pre-arranged meeting time) came and went. She no-called and no-showed me. With my board shorts on and a fishing pole in hand, she completely stood me up.

After what felt like an eternity without a message explaining her actions, she finally texted. With seemingly little remorse, she said, "Sorry, got called into work." I replied with a firm message back stating how my time is to be valued and I would appreciate a simple message letting me know sooner next time so I don't wait around like a dufus.

As she now recalls, she was attracted to the confidence and respect I valued. We then made plans for a rain check. I happened to be heading down from my cousin's house in Orlando and was passing by her home in West Palm Beach. We made plans for brunch because that was what timing allowed and because who doesn't love a good brunch. We hit it off right out of the gate at the restaurant. Being the actors/goofballs we both are, we pretended to work for Yelp corporate (a business review website) and got tip-top service plus freebies. That poor server. We learned more about each other and the conversation flowed effortlessly.

As brunch wrapped, I gave her party leftovers (ribs, cake, etc. Weird, yes. But, what the hay, I thought.) from my cousin's house and a sweet kiss-less goodbye. She now credits those leftovers as a key catalyst in the relationship kindness attraction department. I had a Home Depot commercial casting, which I later booked, that I had to attend. I asked if she would want to meet up afterwards for that elusive paddleboard fishing excursion. She was surprisingly free and up for the endeavor. I also had a rental car and needed to drop it off in Fort Lauderdale, so she ended up picking me up at the airport on the way down after I dropped the car.

By the time we got to my house in Hollywood, Florida, it was too late for paddle boarding. So, we opted for riding beach cruisers to Margaritaville. After making balloon hats with a girl on stilts (true story), we rode over to the Taco Beach Shack. We listened to live music, danced, and laughed.

As we biked home, bliss was found. Nothing but good vibes. We practically hung out with each other all day. Eight separate locations and activities. Never a dull moment or a lapse in conversation. It just felt so right. We both instantly knew something was different. It was a bit scary. Our theme throughout the initial couple of interactions and months to follow was, "Don't fight it." Naturally, our human nature says to protect yourself and keep your wall up. Don't let the other person know your true feelings. It's a game we all have played or probably taught to play. But, when we instilled this concept of "Don't fight it," we just let ourselves and our emotions be free. No games.

We both fell hard. We even waited for intimacy. Something I wasn't accustomed to doing. It just felt like we should wait until the perfect time. We didn't want to "ruin" it. We allowed our friendship to build and to really get to know each other. As we say, we f*cked each other's *minds* far before anything else. We connected on a deep spiritual level. I knew that she was it from the very beginning. I was scared to let her know. But, I knew.

I share this story of how I found love, not to rub it in to anyone who hasn't found it yet, but rather to outline some things that allowed the love to manifest. To start, you must love yourself. You have to be in a state of self-love before you can expect someone else to love you. I have seen this many times with friends of mine. They are not happy with themselves, who or where they are, and in a rampant search for love in order to fill that missing void. The problem is their internal insecurities and negative energy is unconsciously exuding. You have to be in a place of peace and love internally to attract the "right person". Be the person you wish to attract. If you want someone who is kind, intelligent, can take a joke, lives each moment, is driven and motivated to achieve, then be it for yourself!

Live with this mentality and I can say with near certainty that you will find the person you desire. Another thing, when you find that love, don't let it go.

ACTIONABLE TAKEAWAY

The grass may look greener on the other side, but it often isn't. The grass is greener where you water it! Care for, fertilize, water, maintain, and enjoy your own grass… and don't worry about anyone else's.

In relationships, we always can compare and despair to others. We see Joe Schmo and Cindy Lou who post all of their extravagant vacays and date nights on the Gram. We think to ourselves, "Why isn't my relationship like that?" Well, it could be if you take 100% accountability! If you want your relationship to work, take responsibility. Do the little things like make dinner, clean the dishes, and pamper your significant other. Lead by example and they will come around. Most often then not, they will recognize your extra efforts and actions and rise to the occasion. Now, give it sufficient time and effort. But truthfully, there are times when it is in both party's best interest to separate and that's okay too.

As mentioned earlier in this Alignment, here is the rule I go by, and one you might want to as well: If your relationship is in a state of happiness and love 80% of the time, it is healthy. Remember, you can now track this using your Love Calendar. With 80% happiness, you can get that ratio to a more favorable 90% of happiness and love. Below that, it may be time to prioritize change.

Remember, if you want a 10, be a 10. You must be the 10 you seek. It starts with you. Healthy love takes effort and energy. It takes time and commitment. It takes trust and honesty.

Fire's still burning….

But, oh is the juice worth the squeeze! Now get out there and Happy Hustle your loving relationships, my friend!

HAPPY HUSTLE HACK

Whether you're happily married or single and looking for love, this exercise can help! Create the **"The Perfect Partner Page"** where you write in extreme detail exactly who you want to attract. The more detail the better. So get out a piece of paper or your note-taking device and identify the following in your perfect partner (In no particular order):

- **Personality traits** (Overall vibe, what type of person they are.)
- **Looks** (Height, weight, body characteristics, eye color, hair color, shoe size, etc.)
- **Style** (How do they dress and show up?)
- **Sense of Humor** (Funny, jokester, good sport etc.)
- **Interests** (What draws their attention?)
- **Hobbies** (Sports, art, martial arts, etc. What do they like to do?)
- **Morals** (The core values they stand behind.)
- **Faith** (What do they believe in?)
- **Profession** (What they do for work?)
- **Family** (What's their family like? Mom, dad, brothers, sisters, etc.)
- **Kids Preferences** (How many? Boys, girls, both?)
- **Location** (Where they are from?)
- **Political Views** (What is their political stance?)
- **Conflict Resolution** (How they handle conflict.)
- **Long-Term Vision/Goals** (Who they want to become and what they wish to accomplish.)
- **Anything else you can think of**.... (Seriously, go deep.)

You must first get clear on who exactly you want to attract in order to manifest it. Even if you're in a relationship, have your partner go through the exercise with you and each create your Perfect Partner page. Then, if you feel called, respectfully share it with one another. Thus, generating transparency on a whole new level. Then, you can each work to become the partner one another's soul seeks. I know it seems a bit of an overkill. I'm telling ya, spend the time, write this out, and watch yourself manifest the perfect partner! Just like shooting a bow & arrow, you have to identify the target before hitting the bullseye!

In the meantime, if you are single and manifesting your perfect partner, I recommend limiting the time spent dating or hooking up with those you know aren't a good fit. Conserve & protect your energy. Focus on becoming the best version of yourself. Be the 10.

EMBARRASSING FUN FACT

Before meeting my fiancé (at the time of this writing), I was practicing abstinence. I just came off a bender in Southeast Asia and needed time to focus on myself. And wouldn't you know it, after a couple of months of practicing pure self-love and creating my perfect partner page, I connected with the love of my life!

POWERFUL RESOURCES

Books:
The 5 Love Languages by Gary Chapman
The Mastery of Love by Don Miguel Ruiz

Podcasts:
Oprah's Super Soul Conversations
The Happy Hustle Podcast with Steph Hernandez, Episode 46, 114, 160

Movie:
The Notebook

ALIGNMENT 5
MINDFUL SPIRITUALITY

" IF YOU WANT REAL LIFE, REAL GROWTH, REAL SPIRITUALITY, IT'S ALL ABOUT LETTING GO."
-MICKEY SINGER

Just Do Something Dammit... Be Present, Be Grateful, Be Still

As a part of a blissfully balanced life, you must incorporate mindful spirituality. Light an incense, rub a crystal, and flick on that salt lamp, we're going in.

Let me start by asking – Are you spiritual? Do you believe in God or a higher power? Having a "spiritual mindset" is not exclusive to one religion or another. It is for everyone from everywhere. We can all tap into a higher power and even lean on it in times of adversity. I believe in God, not one denomination or another, but a divine source. I grew up with a Catholic father and a Jewish mother. We didn't go to church religiously (pun intended). But when we did, we went to a non-denominational church called the Center for Positive Living. I learned to love every one of all colors and religions, to trust that everything happens for a reason, to understand and accept that we all have a purpose, and to believe in something greater than myself. I still believe most of that to be true. However, I take everything I learn, especially regarding religion, with a grain of salt. What's important for me more so than any particular religion is to have faith and strong morals.

Maybe this is important for you as well? I pray at nearly every meal and I say my gratitudes for all that I have been blessed with every morning and night. That faith is what matters to me. Having a spiritual mindset coupled with distinct values to stand behind allows me to vibrate at a higher frequency, and it can allow you to do the same.

In order to truly become a Happy Hustler, you must practice some form of mindfulness regularly.

This is essential to achieve inner peace and balance. Especially given the craziness of the modern world today. We all need to take the time to tap into our higher selves and connect with a greater power.

Now, I could probably write a whole book on mindfulness and spirituality. Many others have. Some of my favorites are listed at the end of this chapter in the resource section. But, what I want to do is give you the straight to the chase Happy Hustle version to raise your spiritual vibration.

Learning how to surrender and find flow could be one of the more powerful habits (yes, habits) to develop in your current reality. Instead of being tense, resisting what is happening for you (not to you), fighting for your way, or how you assumed it should go down, do something else.

Try this: Surrender. Accept what is taking place and find gratitude for it. Whatever it is, surrender and flow. Again, the only thing you can control is your attitude and effort. Don't stress or worry about things out of your control. Find the silver lining and learn from the experience while flowing with the river of life.

Be Present

Some say there is no past, there is no future, there is only the eternal present. Life is about being the fullest expression of yourself in every moment. Do you suppress your true self given the environment and people in it? Of course, you do. We all do. When we can own who we are and live unapologetically in the eternal present moment, only then can we Happy Hustle freely.

We can appreciate the short seconds that make up the minutes that make up the hours that make up the days that make up our life. Tune into the present today. It is a constant practice.

I still judo chop myself back to the moment on the reg. It is a constant, lovingly fierce internal battle for all of us. Never declaring victory, but only advancing our position.

Attitude of Gratitude

All of these concepts and practices will work to raise your spiritual vibration. However, without this key ingredient (I know, back to the recipe analogy) your life stew is going to taste like poo.

Gratitude, my friend. Do you want to Happy Hustle a life of passion, purpose, and positive impact? Well, develop an attitude of gratitude. That means actually changing your brain's biological response system.

A National Institute of Health study found that when you express kindness or feel gratitude, your hypothalamus floods your brain and releases dopamine and serotonin. These are the two crucial neurotransmitters responsible for our emotions and they make us feel 'good'. They enhance our mood immediately, making us feel happy from the inside.

See, it's scientifically proven that actively practicing an attitude of gratitude makes you happier. Don't waste another moment. Habitually instill gratitude into your everyday life. Find gratitude for everything you have and everything you don't. For example, if you have a roof over your head, food in the fridge, and reliable transportation, find gratitude. If you don't have any missing limbs or life-threatening diseases, find gratitude. Consciously find and list your gratitudes every day and make it a part of your routine.

Seat of Character

The mental and moral qualities distinctive to you are what make up your character. The trick is to ride on a seat of character that positively reflects who you are. And to do so constantly. Practice not allowing other people's intentions or actions to dictate your decisions. Instead, choose to always operate with integrity that is true to you. I am definitely not perfect nor do I claim to be. But, I've since changed my corrupt ways and now operate with full integrity. I always strive to do the 'right thing'. Determine clear morals, things that are non-negotiable in your life. Define attributes for how to behave such as positive energy, hard work, selfless giving, etc. You can then base your decisions on these morals that you live by.

In life, your judgment will for sure be questioned. You will have to make countless decisions between what is 'right' and what is 'wrong'. People will push you in directions and attempt to influence and coerce you. I have made countless 'wrong' decisions. Numerous times, I have operated with a lack of integrity and every time I do, I feel it. I feel it in my core. Like the time when I took something that wasn't mine or got in a barroom brawl. By the time you know you should have made a different choice, many times, it is too late. The deed is done, or being done. I've learned from it and moved forward. I now ride on my seat of character that reflects who I am and who I want to be, every day, as much as I can. With integrity, life is so much better. Think about how you can reflect more closely on who you are and who you want to be by operating with character in each and every action. If you want to take it even a step further, think about how you would want yourself to act 10 years from now. Ask yourself truly, who do you want to be in 10 years? Act like that. Be that person today.

Stillness

Get still more. Slow it the F down, partner. Just chill in the still. Spend time every day being still, quiet, and just chill in the still. Enough said.

Alignment or Misalignment

A super woke friend of mine and creator of The Light Beings community, Kevin Walton, believes that life is an exploration of unlimited creative potential. It is not about being right, wrong, making mistakes, or succeeding. Life is only about living in alignment or misalignment with your true self.

You mean, we've been complicating the shit out of life this whole time? Yep. I know when I first heard of this concept, my mind had a little explosion of awakening. I had previously been caught up with what I should be doing, my goals and their achievement, and the desire to progress. But, when I realized I was doing it all out of alignment, I had no choice but to kick myself in the proverbial gonads and change my ways. What are you doing that is out of alignment?

Meditation

Another way life can be Happy Hustled is with regular meditation. Meditation is vital to the mind, body, and spirit. It allows your soul to shine and your mind to rest. There is so much good that comes from meditating it is no wonder why the majority of the world's ancient philosophers, successful leaders, entrepreneurs, athletes, and stars take time alone to find their inner zen—from Oprah to Tom Brady to Ray Dalio.

Let me preface this section by saying that I am far from a meditation expert. I haven't gone full monk-mode for a year in Tibet, yet. I haven't done a 7-day solo silent retreat in a dark cave in the middle of California. I haven't even meditated every day since I started writing this book. Guilty. I miss a day here and there. What I have done, though, is notice how much happier and grounded I feel when I meditate. Calm, cool, collected like a cucumber in the fridge veggie drawer. Ain't nothing gonna kill my vibe after I zen out.

Take a moment now to reflect. Focus on nothing but your breath and clear your mind as much as possible. Inhale deeply through your nose. Exhale fully through your mouth. It only takes 6 deep breaths to change your state. So, do that now and feel the shift.

There are many different ways to meditate. So, don't feel bad or wrong in your process as each is unique to you. If your mind wanders in the midst of meditation, then congratulations, you're normal. Just gently guide your thoughts back to your breath and get back in that zen-like state.

I personally enjoy meditating in the mornings outside either on the beach or in the wilderness, depending on where I am at the given time. It is an unbelievably beautiful and humbling way to start the morning. Being one with nature, the waves, the wind, the sun, and the endless ocean helps put everything in perspective. If you don't live near the beach, just go outside.

Studies show we spend nearly 96% of our time indoors. Whenever possible, get outside, breathe fresh air, get natural sunlight, ground yourself to Mother Earth, and enjoy the moment. You may find that what seems so essential may be quite insignificant in the scheme of things. The stress that weighs on us can be released. Life's problems, both big and small, can be paused for the time being. Also, we can focus on our breath.

Engaging all of our senses and just being present can have profound effects on your happiness.

Listen, whatever you do, you owe it to yourself to have a meditation practice and breath work actively in your daily routine. I encourage you to look up Wim Hof if you want to deep dive into the wonders of breathwork. Don't overcomplicate it. Just get still and quiet for 5-10 minutes, at least, and focus on your breathing. That's it! Just start with that. Of course, you can take it to higher levels and increase the duration. Even just that 5 minutes a day will make a huge difference on your Happy Hustlin' journey to balanced greatness.

Surrender The Soul

After traveling to the Temple of the Universe in Alachua Florida and meditating with the great Mickey Singer, I learned a lot about myself, life, and spirituality. Mickey Singer is a NYT best-selling author of The Untethered Soul and The Surrender Experiment and co-founder of what is now WebMD. The Temple of the Universe is a yogi's heaven with wide-open, beautiful rolling green hills, thick massive trees scattered throughout the property, birds chirping, animals playing, old Florida feel. Untouched at its finest. It's the perfect place to tap into oneself and the mind.

Stillness and calm exude over the 200+ acre property. The temple itself, a wooden cabin-like building built by Mickey himself back in the 70's with a soft carpet flooring where everyone sits, candles placed throughout, and pictures of spiritual gurus hanging on all of the walls. Mediations and teachings are free and he welcomes guests of all kinds for group meditations and teachings throughout the week at specific times. More on Mickey below in the Happy Hustler Spotlight.

Be You, Be True

Always be unapologetically yourself. All jokes aside, this is a game-changer. Being transparent and real are the most appreciated qualities in this world full of false digital identities. Know who you are as a human, what you stand for, and what you're willing to fight for. Know that your opinion of yourself is what matters most. And know that you will never regret being true to your soul.

There are many times when I do things that are wacky and out there, unapologetically me. For example, I usually compete in the Miami Model Beach

Volleyball tournament every year. This tournament comprises the top 12 modeling agencies in Miami going head-to-head, battling for beach bragging rights. My attire each year is themed and unique. This past year, I wore an American Flag Speedo, American Flag Vest, and American Flag visor to represent the ole' USA. The second day, I wore a camouflage get-up including a camo speedo, camo neck bandana, and camo bucket hat. I was pretty much the only one out there, out of hundreds of the most beautiful models gathered, wearing anything of the sort. The point is not to go out there and rock a speedo. Although, kudos to you if you do. The point is to just be you and give less fucks about what other people think.

Pre-game stretches at Miami Model Beach Volleyball on South Beach in my limited camo attire.

When I was growing up, I remember how embarrassed I felt when I would be out with my mom at a restaurant and there was a live band. She would always be the first one on the dance floor out there getting it, without caring what people thought. She would light up the place with her 1970's dance moves and natural glow. I honestly didn't start appreciating the self-confidence she demonstrated time and time again until I was far out of my teens. She was not trying to impress anyone. She was just having fun and being unapologetically herself. Life can be short, don't waste a second trying to be anyone but you.

However you do it, identify as many things about your personality as you can. Pinpoint the pure happiness and determine how to grow those moments. Live fully as YOU, without regrets. Meditate, have faith, and employ a spiritual mindset. Life's better when you do.

HAPPY HUSTLER SPOTLIGHT

Mickey Ginger

Mickey is one of the most unique individuals I've ever met. I had the honor of building a relationship with him thanks to my brother who was one of his mentees all throughout his time attending the University of Florida. Mickey is an old yogi with a low grey ponytail, glasses, usually rocking a collared, basic colored shirt, and khaki pants. He built a multi-million-dollar company all from his shack in the woods in the middle of Florida. For those of you who don't know him, I highly recommend reading his books.

He was interviewed multiple times by Oprah and Tony Robbins and is one of the most awakened beings I've ever met. At first contact with Mickey, you can tell he's different. He truly owns his uniqueness and is unapologetically himself. He has a way of captivating a crowd with his charisma, often cracking jokes mid-meditation. At the Temple of the Universe we discuss various topics. But none more earth-shattering to my own personal psyche than the one I want to share with you now.

Steph & I at Mickey's Temple of the Universe in Florida.

Mickey says, "Think of your mind as a house. Many of us have a completely messy house. Oftentimes, this place is filthy, dust in every corner, dirt on the floors, nothing is organized nor put away... I mean, shit everywhere. Not to mention there are holes in the actual foundation and termites are rotting its core. Ask yourself, how clean is your house? Do you have negative thoughts acting as termites eating away throughout your day? Do you stress yourself out about work or family drama that doesn't serve you? If someone cuts you off in traffic or honks at you, do you lose your cool? Think of all the melodramatic thoughts we put in our minds or what we create from nothing. All of these reactions and thoughts are reflections of our mind's state. We have to clean it up and remove the obstacles. Much like we have to clean our actual houses, we have to clean up and provide some TLC to our mind and body, our Temple. We have to relax and release."

Besides the concept of cleaning up our messy houses, one of the most valuable concepts I've learned from Mickey is the idea and exquisite articulation of the little voice inside our heads. We all have one. And a lot of times, this thing won't shut up! It hoots and hollers about everything and anything.

In order to truly enjoy the journey and hustle for our happiness, we must learn to quiet the voice. Or, at the least control it. "Are you okay?" That is what Mickey asks. After all, we are but a microscopic speck sitting on a floating rock orbiting a star somewhere in the middle of the universe. What makes you soooo not okay that your little voice has to remind you constantly? Put it all into perspective.

When you begin to notice the voice inside your head and recognize that it is not you, then you will start to be 'okay'. You are not your head, nor your heart, nor your thoughts, you are the one noticing! Wake up, my friend. Realize that this is the reality. Stop the preferred suffering. Don't make up stories with limiting beliefs any longer. Know that you can handle this. Don't overcomplicate life and happiness. Be okay inside your head.

You can conquer your thoughts. You can be 'okay' wherever you are. You can find happiness in the hustle of achieving what you desire. You don't have to wait until you get there. You can be Happy Hustlin' on the journey at every step of the way. As Mickey says, clean your house and be okay with what is. And notice who's noticing. You, the real you.

STORY TIME: COMMON AFFINITY & CONNECTEDNESS

Since I was a young boy, I have been practicing and learning the ancient Taoist, or Daoist, healing arts. My mom, who was big into Eastern medicine and methodologies, introduced me to Tai Chi, Qi gong, Kung fu, and the Daoist way.

I was introduced to Master Chen at a very early age. From extreme poverty in rural China to becoming a rising prominent spiritual leader in the West, Master Chen has used the way of the Dao to guide thousands of people to create health, happiness, and harmony.

As a child, he was chosen to be trained by the 5 Elder Daoist Masters in the legendary temples of the sacred Wudang Mountains. The same location where they shot scenes for the newer version of The Karate Kid movie.

Through intensive training in a disciplined environment, Chen learned to master mind, body, and spirit. Chen became his own Master Within by applying Daoism's ancient practices based on thousands of years of observation of the universe and our true nature within it. He then wrote a book with this title!

He left the monastery holding two sacred lineages of knowledge: Long Men Pai and Zhang San Feng Pai.

Master Chen journeyed to the United States in 1990 on a sacred mission to teach Daoist practical philosophies and empower the West to heal the body, mind, and spirit.

I was 12 years old when Master Chen first called me his nephew and took me in as family. Up until that point, I would just sit in the back of the rooms at his lectures and workshops as my mom participated. I was always interested in martial arts, but never fully understood the meaning behind the methods. I can distinctly remember the day when Master Chen came to my house to train my brother and I. We began in the early afternoon by cultivating our Qi energy and learning basic Kung fu kicks and punches. We continued to practice the same moves over and over again until we performed them to Master Chen's satisfaction. My brother Grant became tired and bowed out of training as night fell. I, hungry to learn this ancient wisdom and impress my

Master, was a willing student far until the early hours of the morning. Master Chen and I stayed up all night training, cultivating Qi, moving energy, being still, recognizing our power and our common affinity and connectedness. This night solidified my passion for martial arts. It also confirmed that there was a higher power. That we are spiritual beings and that we must train our minds to connect to source energy.

Steph and I with Master Chen at his Dao House in Estes Park, Colorado.

ACTIONABLE TAKEAWAY

I don't expect an ancient Kung Fu master or Daoist Priest to come to your house to share these lessons with you. **What I do want to share with you is the importance of implementing some type of mindful spiritual practice regularly,** connecting to a higher power in your life, and having faith and morals by which you live by. I am a student of life. All religions are thus another lesson in the curriculum. In order to Happy Hustle a life of Blissful Balance, we mustn't overlook the essence of our spirituality. Believe in something greater than yourself. Live for something more than your personal desires. Mindful spirituality can exponentially increase your happiness and fulfillment along the journey.

"Observe nature, observe yourself, teach yourself." - Master Wu Dang Chen

EMBARRASSING FUN FACT

I often practice with my katana sword in the front yard of my home. Slicing old fruit and vegetables with swift swings is among one of my favorite simple joys. This often begets awkward looks from passersby and neighbors with the occasional police questioning.

Me & my fruit splitting katana... you may be saying "Wow, two shirtless split pictures in one chapter Cary? Bravo sir."

POWERFUL RESOURCES

Books:
The Master Within by Master Wu Dang Chen
The Power by Rhonda Byrne
Conversations with God by Neale Donald Walsh
The Power of Now by Eckhart Tolle

Podcasts:
Jon Gordon Podcast

Movie:
Rewired with Dr. Joe Dispenza

Online Course:
Living from a Place of Surrender- The Untethered Soul in Action by Mickey Singer

ALIGNMENT 6
ABUNDANCE FINANCIALLY

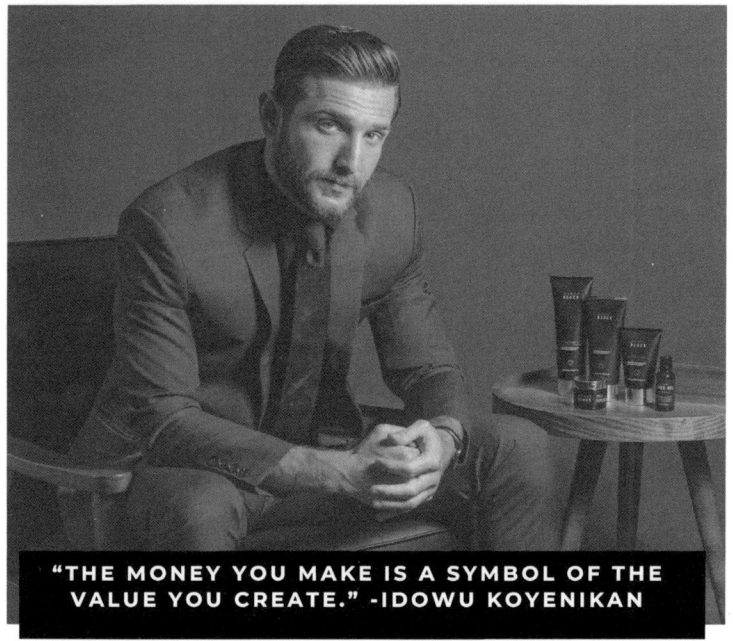

"THE MONEY YOU MAKE IS A SYMBOL OF THE VALUE YOU CREATE." -IDOWU KOYENIKAN

Save, Spend, And Invest Wisely To Achieve Financial Freedom

"Money, money, moneyy, moneeyyyy….. money!" Yes, that classic song from The O'Jays - For the Love of Money was pretty spot on with their lyrics. Some people do good things with it, some people do bad things with it, but everybody's got to have it. As a Happy Hustler, I see money as a tool to help me live a life of passion, purpose, and positive impact. Depending on where you ranked yourself in this Alignment, you're going to want to pay extra attention to this section as money is essential if you truly wish to become a Happy Hustler.

The ability to financially provide and care for your family and loved ones is a goal I'm sure we all possess. Being able to buy and invest in what you want, when you want, with whom you want, is the ultimate financial freedom, right? Well, in order to achieve financial freedom and abundance, it honestly boils down to having and applying financial literacy, in my opinion. Do you spend more than you earn? Do you invest in assets that appreciate or depreciate in value? Do you leverage bank accounts, credit cards, mortgages, "the system" to your advantage? Or, do you just settle for the convenient option? In order to be a Happy Hustler, you need to have your finances in check and educate yourself.

In this chapter, I'll give you a crash course on how I went from 16k in student loan and credit card debt back in my early twenties to debt-free and 20k in savings in less than 12 months. I'll provide you with the resources I used and still use today to live a financially abundant life. One that pulls in well over 6 figures a year on cruise control while not usually working more than 20 hours a week and living a blissfully balanced life. Buckle up, we're going in!

Ignorance is a Choice

First and foremost, let me say that in this day and age, in the world of information readily available at your fingertips, being financially ignorant is a choice. If you do not know the difference between a stock and a bond, what your credit card APR is, the sales tax on every purchase you make, it is only because you have chosen not to educate yourself. That shit ends today. It is time to become financially literate and optimize your finances. With that, you must educate yourself. Buy financial books, subscribe to financial YouTube channels, listen to financial podcasts, and read financial blogs. You have the power to change your financial future and it starts with education. The goal is to learn, create, and implement a foundational system that will work for you for the rest of your life with only minor adjustments along the way as needed.

Spend Smart

You must learn to smartly spend your hard-earned dollars. There are certain things that I don't think twice about spending money on like books. I buy books the instant I am interested in one, whether it be on educational courses, organic food and drinks, or vitamins. I know that by exchanging the paper for the product, that exchange has exponential long term benefits. However, there are other items that I research, analyze, price shop, and compare before even thinking about actually pulling the trigger. Depending on the product, I will determine if it is a 'need' or a 'want' and if that money is better served elsewhere. For example, like investing in my business, Roth IRA, or dividend stocks.

The point being, put everything you wish to purchase through the filter of, "Is this a need or a want? Do I actually need it to enhance my happiness, health, business, or overall well-being?"

Or is it just a want? Meaning, you could do without it and be just fine. Now, I'm not saying don't treat yourself. Heck, I love a swag pair of shoes and a fancy dinner just as much as the next guy. But, until you have your finances in check and a system in place where you actually know your numbers (ie: weekly budget, amount invested, debt, bills, etc.) keenly evaluate all of your purchases. Once you have financial stability and abundance, you can set aside $500 to spend on yourself, then you can do so guilt-free. Until then, every dollar spent now could be worth two tomorrow. So, spend smart. The Money Value Over Time (MVOT) is a real calculation in which you must consider. With inflation, opportunity cost, and MVOT, each dollar that you spend costs you more than you actually think. Without going too deep into the weeds here, just recognize that you must spend smart if you wish to achieve financial abundance.

Save

Saving money every month is not only a solid idea, it is a necessity in order to become financially free. Even if you just set up your main bank account (I use Charles Schwab) to deposit $150 a month to your separate savings account (I use Capital One 360 savings), the power of compound interest over time will be quietly working in the background. In order to save, you must start. They say the best time to start was 10 years ago and the second best time is today.

Start now! Even if you feel you don't have the liquid capital to save thousands, save hundreds instead. If you can't save hundreds this month, skip the dinner out and morning coffee and save $50. If possible, create multiple savings accounts: one emergency fund (just in case), one retirement fund (for you as an old-timer to enjoy), and one personal savings (for investments, houses, cars, business, etc.). Save today and free your future self. You won't regret it.

Invest

Investing is a whole other animal than simply saving. They say the 3 main ways to get wealthy, not just rich, are:

- **Start a successful business**
- **Buy real estate assets and leverage them effectively**
- **Invest wisely in the stock market**

I'm not a financial guru by any means, nor do I claim to be, but I have been able to take what I've learned and successfully invest in the stock market. For the most part, my initial investments compound year after year. The major mindset shift I made in order to do so was taking accountability for myself and my investments.

I didn't hire a financial advisor to manage my portfolio. Although, I have consulted with multiple. Instead, I vetted the company's stocks and did it myself. Many "financial experts" don't know their ass from their elbow when it comes to predicting the market so don't get played. Heck, no one really knows for certain. Most just make predictions and get lucky from time to time. With that being said, if you don't have the time to manage your own money and you do decide to go the financial advisor route, make sure to get personal references, research the company they work for and which private interests they may be beholden to.

There are some tried and true investment principles that can help guide your decisions. I recommend reading two books that will help you become financially literate and understand the market.

I Will Teach You to Be Rich by Ramit Sethi

This is the best book I have ever read regarding money. It gives you a practical step-by-step system via a 6-week program that will transform your finances. He is also funny and shares tons of reader success stories who have changed their lives by applying his teachings.

Money Master the Game by Tony Robbins

Tony interviews some of the greatest minds in the financial and wealth management game. He gives actionable steps to investing, saving, earning, and much more. You will further understand the market and the proven and tested principles of investing.

Automate Your $$ Machine

The real key is to automate your finances so that the system works while you sleep. The goal is to wake up on the first of the month and a series of digital events has taken place inside your accounts, allocating your money in the best possible way.

This takes time. But, it is more than possible. It is essential in order to Happy Hustle your dream reality. Read the books I have recommended above and implement the lessons ASAP.

Use Technology

Personal Capital
A solid web-based platform that allows you to see your financial well-being in its entirety. You can connect all of your accounts and credit cards so that you know your exact net worth, debts, etc. at any given moment. You can also create budgets and leverage many other solid features for managing your money. I highly recommend using this software to help keep your finances in check.

Acorns
A great app that automatically invests and manages your money for you. You set the risk level and how much you want it to automatically withdraw from your checking account. Each withdrawal is allocated to your investments and it does the work for you. You can also set it so that it rounds up a portion of every dollar you spend.

For instance, if you buy a cup of coffee for $2.60, that remaining .40 cents will be sent to the investment account to be allocated to your investment portfolio. You can also double and triple your round-ups. It's an easy way to get in the market and have your money work for you with an automated system.

All in all, when it comes to Happy Hustlin' your dreams into reality, money has to be a part of the conversation. Depending on where you ranked yourself in the "Are you a Happy Hustler Assessment" (1-5), take stock and prioritize change accordingly. You must educate yourself and become financially literate. I can tell you with certainty that if you don't have this Alignment in check, meaning you're not Happy Hustlin' Abundance Financially, your entire existence will be filled with much more stress and

and anxiety. Living in debt, paycheck to paycheck, coupon cutting, and price shopping may have been (or currently is) a part of your journey as it was mine. However, it does not have to dictate your future financial success. Choose to Happy Hustle your finances today.

Set up a system to spend, save, and invest wisely and educate yo-self! Take full accountability for your current financial status. Learn from your past mistakes and make better financial decisions from this day forward. It's time to Happy Hustle that moolah, mi amigo!

I learned more about business and finances in the first 6 months of starting a company than I did in 4 years of college. Point being, take accountability for your financial education. Here is a rare pic of my immediate family together from my college graduation.

HAPPY HUSTLER SPOTLIGHT

Tony Robbins

Tony Robbins is not only one of the most influential human beings on Planet Earth, but he is for sure a Happy Hustler. Tony Robbins is an entrepreneur, #1 NY Times best-selling author, philanthropist, and the nation's #1 life and business strategist. For more than 4 decades, over 50 million people have enjoyed the warmth, humor, and transformational power of his business and personal development events. I personally have been to multiple Tony Robbins seminars from Unleash the Power Within to Business Mastery, read his books, and listened to his audio programs. He has had a massive impact on my life and has inspired me on my journey. In addition to selling out his own seminars and events, Tony is the chairman of a holding company of more than 50 privately held businesses with a combined sales exceeding $6 billion per year. The guy knows the importance of financial literacy and creating a system that accrues wealth. And since he is financially abundant, he has turned to giving to others. He once said, "The secret to living is giving," which has stuck with me ever since. Through his philanthropic partnership with Feeding America, Mr. Robbins has provided over 500 million meals in the last 5 years to those in need. He has also initiated programs in more than 1,500 schools, 700 prisons, and 50,000 service organizations and shelters. He has lived an extraordinary life and is a leader amongst leaders, coaching 3 US Presidents, billionaires, Fortune 500 CEOs, professional athletes, musicians, actors, and everyone in between. I could go on and on about Tony's accomplishments. The point I want to make that is most relevant to this chapter is that he has his finances on point and seeks wisdom from those wiser than him regarding money. He invests regularly and has an automated system that grows his fortune while he sleeps. And you can too! He is definitely a Happy Hustler worth following and I am grateful for all he has taught me.

STORY TIME: HOW I MADE A $25,000 SALE ON A BEACH-SIDE ZOOM CALL AND HOW YOU CAN TOO

I closed a $25,000 sale on a Zoom call while sipping fresh jugo de coco sitting on the beach with my lovely lady beside me in a sexy red bikini. We're in a rural surf town somewhere in the middle of Guatemala where surprisingly their WiFi was quite strong. It took me roughly 50 minutes in total on the call to establish the rapport, figure out his wants and needs, build the belief, and present an opportunity to join our biohacking health and performance optimization coaching program.

Steph & I hanging poolside at our Guatemalan pad, living true to lifestyle entrepreneurship.

Ahh, lifestyle entrepreneurship at its finest. This was one of those moments that I had dreamed about. Making money, while making an impact, while enjoying my life! Blissfully balanced and straight Happy Hustlin'.

See, one of the quickest ways you can make more money right away is by learning effective sales techniques. Sales are the lifeblood of any business. Increase your sales and you'll make more money. It's as simple as that.

One of the ways that I was able to get out of $16K in credit card debt and have over $20K in savings in less than 12 months was by sharpening my sales sword. I fully realize this isn't a "business book" and we're talking about Happy Hustlin' a balanced life in the 10 Alignments. In order to help you Happy Hustle your Abundance Financially, sales secrets must be shared. If you take away nothing else from this book (which should be near impossible) but how to increase your sales, I know this will positively impact your life. That is how important sales are to your success.

In lieu of true story time, I'm going to give you a quick crash course in some of the most successful sales strategies that I have used to sell over a million dollars in the last two years alone while working less than 20 hours per week. And no, I'm not talking about slimy, scammy, hard closing sales. I'm talking about actually helping people by selling as a service that adds value to their life.

Whether you are selling online coaching, courses, books, live events, a physical product, physical service, or something in between, these sales tactics will be applicable.

But first, I want to give credit where credit is due. I have learned some of these sales tactics and strategies from my superb sales friends: Mr. Eli Wilde, #1 sales producer for Tony Robbins who has sold over 9 figures at the time of this writing. Mr. Randy Grizzle, OG salesman and founder of Closer Secrets, who sold over 25 million by phone for Russell Brunson and Clickfunnels. Check out episode 11 on the Happy Hustle Podcast where I interviewed Randy on *Mastering your Money and High-Ticket Sales Process.* And lastly, Mr. Rory Vaden, New York Times best-selling author and Hall of Fame speaker who also ran an 8-figure sales organization. Check out episode 42 on the Happy Hustle Podcast where I interviewed Rory on *Building an Influential Personal Brand.*

I am going to share with you some of the greatest lessons that I've learned from these individuals. I'll share a talk track for you to crush your sales meetings whether by phone, Zoom, or in-person. I'll add in my own unique ninja sales kicks that I learned from selling myself as professional model/actor on thousands of auditions. I'll also include the sales tactics I used to digitally close $25k+ sales in 45 minutes time and time again. You will learn how you can too. Saddle up, it's time for a sales rodeo.

#1 Rule of Sales

LISTEN. Listening is legit your greatest asset as a salesperson. If you ask your prospect the right questions, they will give you the answers. All you have to do is just listen. Don't overcomplicate this. Find out what they want by actually listening to them. Then, use their exact language and verbiage when presenting your offer to help fulfill their needs and get them their desired result. This should go without saying, make sure you stand 100% behind whatever product or service you're selling or don't sell it.

Pressure-Free Persuasion

Be the facilitator of a conversation that guides your prospect into making the best decision for them, even if that decision means you will not close a sale. If you have your prospect's best interest in mind, you are going to substantially increase your sales closing percentage. Come from a place of integrity and service. Build a relationship with your prospect. Don't pressure them, but rather provide them with firm, direct questions to guide their decision. Indecision is thy enemy so your goal is to get them to make a decision, be it a yes or a no. More on this soon.

Emotion vs Logic

People buy with emotion but justify with logic. Meaning, you must appeal to their emotional state throughout the sales process by painting the picture of what is possible for them. Then, you equally must justify that with logical sense. This often means doing the math. Showing them that X amount of dollars invested with you will equal a return on their investment of X amount of potential dollars. Always do the math and share the numbers. Make sure to mention the opportunity cost of not buying.

Indecision is the Enemy

Let's face it, people need help making decisions. People get stuck in analysis paralysis and freeze. People will often procrastinate, especially when attempting to make a larger purchase. Your job as a salesperson is to be a professional decision-making helper. Whether it's a yes or a no, both should be counted as a win. The real loss is indecision. If you can actually help them with your product or service and you let them leave the conversation with no decision or clear follow-up plan, you are doing the prospect a disservice. Seriously, help them make a decision either one way or another to avoid the depths of indecision despair.

Built-In Objection Busters

Everyone has objections. Figure out what the 5 main objections are for your product or service. Throughout your pitch/conversation, bake them in organically so you are naturally busting their beliefs. Usually, it comes down to time, money, their spouse, etc. However, people are resourceful folk. So if they really want it, 9 times out of 10 they can overcome even the deepest objections with resourcefulness. Help them by busting their objections and show them a way through.

Talk Track

Whether you are selling on the phone, over a video call, or in person, a talk track can be utilized to increase your sales conversion rate. Create one customized for you and your business. Do not skip steps. Each step builds upon the other. Listen and take notes. Here is an example of a more generalized talk track that can be used in its entirety or takes pieces of it. Compliments a la Cary. Happy Selling!

Happy Hustle Hack: The 7 Steps to Selling

1. Build the Rapport
Start by finding out more about them. Ask where they are based. Give an honest compliment. Make small talk. Your first initial 30 to 60 seconds of the interaction will often dictate the overall vibe and, ultimately, the sales call success. Make a good first impression.

2. Find the Pain & Obstacle
Ask them why you're talking today. Figure out what is holding them back. What are they struggling with? What is their weakness? What are they looking for help with? Find the pain in their life.

3. Identify the Dream, the Want, and the Why
Figure out what they actually want. Identify what their dream is and determine why they want what they want. This is crucial. Make sure you clearly know this as you will be using it later in the convo.

4. Demonstrate Future Success & Show Story of What's Possible
Now that you know what's holding them back and where they want to go, you can clearly identify if what you have to offer is going to help get them there. If so, demonstrate their future success with your product or service. Use past stories of other similar clients who have used your product or service and achieved results. People need case studies and social proof to know it is possible for them. Showcase their successes and paint the picture for them.

5. Qualify Properly
Before presenting the opportunity, you want to make sure that this prospect is qualified for your product or service in order to ensure results. This could mean that you have criteria in which you only work with certain client traits. Don't skip this step. Make sure you are serving those in which you know you can get results for. That is how you will build word-of-mouth referrals. You should know your perfect target customer and sell to them specifically. If it's not a fit or they don't qualify, walk away from the sale and be okay with that. Oftentimes, selling to the wrong type of clients just ends up causing more problems than it's worth.

6. Create Ethical Urgency and Scarcity

This step can either be your greatest ally or your worst enemy. This step is the key to ETHICAL scarcity and urgency; meaning, not made up. People often need a push to take action. You can give them the necessary incentive by creating ethical urgency and scarcity. That could mean a limited number of spots in your program, offering only a certain number of products in limited quantities, or potentially offering them a valuable bonus for signing up on the call. This step is crucial in order to close on the same day and avoid the response, "I need to sleep on it" or "Let me think about it and get back to you". I like to structure a three-hour window with my sales calls by stating, "I need a decision yes or no three hours after our call ends in order to get X bonus incentive or a spot in the program".

7. Congratulate and Present Opportunity

If it is a fit, congratulate them and present them with the opportunity to purchase your product or service. Desperate salespeople don't sell. Frame the sale as the opportunity that it is. Know that you can get the results in whatever they are lacking or struggling with and congratulate them with genuine excitement. Ask the question, "Is there any reason you wouldn't take action and get started today?" If there are still objections, figure out what those are and how to alleviate them. I often like to bring up their dream and their pain points. I re-state that it *is* possible for them and I am certain that the product or service will help them. Thus, giving them peace of mind and the reassurance to take immediate action. That is essentially the talk track that you can use to close discovery calls, in-person meetings, zoom calls, you name it. The steps are universal.

One final sales note: Be Yourself

One of the best ways I've found to actually sell myself and the product or service at hand is to be authentically me. You cannot be authentically me. You can only be authentically you. So, keep it real and be transparent. People's bullshit meters are super high. They can detect a snake in the grass. Don't be that person. Just Happy Hustle your sales in a way that you would want your own mom or dad to be sold to. Operate with respect and integrity and you'll be on your way to Abundance Financially, my friend. Just make sure your margins are in check. Know your numbers and actually make money on the products and services that you're selling. ;)

ACTIONABLE TAKEAWAY

So, there you have it. Sales are your escalator to Abundance Financially. **Learn how to sell more effectively and you can have it all in your life.** Financial freedom and abundance is more than possible for you. This is specially true if you follow the lessons in this chapter: spend, save, and invest wisely!

EMBARRASSING FUN FACT

I've physically sold myself on multiple occasions... One time, immediately after watching Magic Mike, I thought I could hack it as a Chicago bachelorette party dancer. Channing just made it look so fun and easy. Let me tell you, it's not. I'm not going to elaborate, but let's just say things got weird, lol. That was the first and last bachelorette party I ever did.

POWERFUL RESOURCES

Books:
I Will Teach You to Be Rich by Ramit Sethi
Money Master the Game by Tony Robbins
Rich Dad Poor Dad by Robert Kiyosaki
Tax-Free Wealth by Tom Wheelwright

Podcasts:
Peter Schiff Show

Youtube:
ValueTainment by Patrick Bet-David
Rich Dad Channel by Robert Kiyosaki

Movie:
The Big Short

ALIGNMENT 7
PERSONAL DEVELOPMENT

"FORMAL EDUCATION WILL MAKE YOU A LIVING.
SELF-EDUCATION WILL MAKE YOU A FORTUNE."
- JIM ROHN

Learn Something Everyday
Grow & Evolve or Shrink & Dissolve

We're going to kick things off by clearly stating the sheer importance of learning something new every day. If you are not growing and evolving, you are shrinking and dissolving. I know it sounds dramatic, but we must prioritize our personal growth. Where did you rank yourself in this Alignment (1-5)? If it's not a 5, then you have some room to improve. Heck, we all do. When you apply the following insights from this section, this is one Alignment that can instantly have a positive effect. So, get ready to grow!

Do you have a system to ensure your personal growth? To truly be a Happy Hustler, you need to be learning and acquiring new skills every day. Even if that is just reading 15 pages or listening to a self-improvement podcast. Hint: The Happy Hustle Podcast is a solid choice. ;) It all adds up to consistent personal growth. We naturally have evolved as human beings from ancient cave dwellers to modern technologists all because of personal development. Although some might argue that consuming psychedelic mushrooms were a trigger for our rapid cognitive evolution, A.K.A. the Stoned Ape Theory. This is neither here nor there, but an interesting thought.

The point being, this growth is rooted in skill acquisition. I know you have a ton of shit on your plate, but that is no excuse to not advance yourself and develop your skills. From learning copywriting to learning a new language, from mastering sales to mastering speed reading, from enhancing your verbal articulation to enhancing your EQ (Emotional Intelligence), each and every skill that you acquire adds value to your life.

You must make time to Happy Hustle for personal growth. This is neither a chore nor a burden. It's an absolute necessity or else a life of meager complacency may be in your future. I created a system that helps me ensure persistent personal development each day. Here's how I do it and how you can too.

The Happy Hustle Growth System

Implement these elements into your routine every day to ensure never-ending personal growth. By the end of it, you will have at least 90 minutes of personal growth added into your daily routine.

Morning - Find 30 minutes of uninterrupted reading time for self-improvement, business, spiritual, or fiction books. No, romantic novels don't count. Feed the mind with positive knowledge. All inspiring, educational content!

Afternoon - Find at least 30 minutes of uninterrupted time to listen to a podcast of your liking. One that inspires, educates, and entertains you. Choose one that is related to your goals.

Evening - Find at least 30 minutes to watch a visually stimulating and educational show, documentary, or movie. I like going on YouTube for this and typing in self-improvement buzzwords. There is a ton of amazing content to choose from. So, just pick items that are relevant to you and your current goals.

Change your habits from getting sucked into a meaningless series to feeding your mind something of value. No more horror movies or crap content that doesn't add value to your life. Opt for content that raises your vibration and helps you grow!

These small changes over time will make a massive difference in your life. Utilize the compound effect. Start now by being extremely diligent as to what you input into your brain. It all matters.

Author's Note: If 90 minutes of personal development 7 days per week feels overwhelming, start with 15-minute blocks of time 5 days per week. Use this time for reading, listening, and watching inspirational educational content. Then, you can build your way up by adding time accordingly. Yes, I'm giving you an out because I want you to actually start implementing this practice into your routine. Better you start small than not start at all. Just start!

Invest in Mentors, Coaches, Courses, Seminars, Conferences, and Yourself

Want to know the real catalyst to expedite your success? Hire experts. Want to learn how to do something in a fraction of the time? Hire a professional in that field.

Set aside a budget each year to invest in your personal growth. That money can be used for attending conferences, hiring mentors or coaches, or investing in educational courses or training... and nothing else.

Me and one of my mentors Russell Brunson at his Inner Circle Mastermind in Boise... A.K.A.: One of the best online marketers in the game and Co-Founder of the 9-figure company, Clickfunnels.

Ask yourself these questions:

- What skill could you acquire to help you expedite your success? Do some research and find someone who possesses that skill and pay them to teach you!
- What conference have you told yourself you should really attend next year? Purchase a ticket now. Don't delay. If money's tight, see if they offer a scholarship or if you can volunteer to work in exchange for entry. There's always a way.

- What professional in your industry do you respect and is currently where you want to be? Do they offer a group coaching program or a 1-on-1 consulting option? If so, then reach out. Book a time to connect and see if it's a fit!
- What course or training could shortcut your learning curve in your business and help you spread your message to the world? Buy it! Don't hesitate.
- Obviously, use discernment with any personal growth purchase as it seems everyone and their mothers are a "guru" these days. My rule: I don't take advice from people I wouldn't honestly trade places with. During my vetting process, I extensively assess their life both personally and professionally. If I wouldn't want to be in their shoes, I find someone else to learn from.

Just know that you are the best investment you will ever make. Start taking this seriously. Happy Hustle your personal growth every single day. It may seem like the time, money, and resources could be better served elsewhere, but I promise you this is not the case. A dollar invested in yourself and your skillset today could be worth 3 dollars next week.

The Happy Hustle Club

As you now know, investing in yourself and surrounding yourself with a like-minded community is imperative for success. Speaking of which, that is why The Happy Hustle Club was created. This community is here to help 6+ figure earning online entrepreneurs implement the S.O.U.L.M.A.P.P.I.N. system. Not just read about it, but *be* about it. Get bi-weekly Balance Building trainings, Guest Guru Happy Hours, Happy Hustle Hot Seats, Selfless Service Sessions, and Cash Accountability Challenges while connecting with other world-class Happy Hustlers. If you're interested in joining THE CLUB, apply today at www.thehappyhustleclub.com.

Delayed gratification is the name of the game, my friend. Realize that investing in yourself will ensure that you are ready and able to seize future opportunities. It will help you create magic otherwise not possible without the tools you've spent years sharpening prior.

So, get on with it and make Alignment #7: Personal Development a daily priority!

As you know, I like to highlight other Happy Hustlers out there who are a shining example of each Alignment. Someone who is Happy Hustlin' a life on their terms and creating a positive impact in the process. The following spotlight is a friend of mine doing just that…

HAPPY HUSTLER SPOTLIGHT

Lewis Howes

Maybe you know Lewis Howes or maybe you don't. I personally started following Lewis online around 2014, before he amassed a successful personal growth business empire. Today, he has touched hundreds of millions of people with his message.

He is a NYT best-selling author, host of a top 10 podcast, entrepreneur, and international motivational speaker. He has connected with the who's who of celebrities because of the platform he created.

He shares his message of "Inspiring Greatness Within" in many forms including coaching programs, masterminds, training, and webinars. Back in 2016, I actually got to interview him for a couple of hours at his West Hollywood apartment for a TV show I was hosting. At the time, I had been a part of his School of Greatness Academy and learned a ton from him and his podcast guests. I was very familiar with his message, his humble Ohio roots, and the ample adversities he faced like sexual abuse and a devasting, career-ending sports injury. We had a great interview.

One thing that stuck out was how much of a priority he makes personal development and investing in his own growth. He is constantly investing in mentors, coaches, training, and conferences. Point is, success leaves clues and this is one of those clues. Invest in yourself!

Lewis never gave up on his dream and neither should you. He is now changing the lives of millions of people all over the world with his content. He is indeed a Happy Hustler and one I am grateful to know.

Lewis and I at his place in West Hollywood after crushing an interview… the handle bar mustache was in full effect, ha.

Shortly after hanging with Lewis, I moved to Bangkok, Thailand. That same handle bar mustache got invited to party in The Hangover 2 Suite where they shot the movie. They thought I was Bradley Cooper (which I get often) and basically rolled out the red carpet. Quite the night, indeed. You may wonder why this is included in the book. Welp, I had extra room on the page and figured you could use a laugh.

STORY TIME: FROM CRAIGSLIST GIGS TO BIG SCREEN BOOKINGS
LESSONS OF OVERCOMING REJECTION AND DIFFERENTIATING YOURSELF FROM THE COMPETITION

One of the most beneficial representations of Happy Hustlin' in the area of personal development is my journey as a professional actor and model. I legit went from sketchy Craigslist gigs to lucrative big-screen bookings. At the time of this writing, I have been acting and modeling for over 15 years. I now dabble more casually as a profitable side hobby. At one point, I was doing the damn thang at the highest level.

This journey was one filled with personal growth and development, learning each day how to become a better version of myself, and ultimately how to become a better actor and model. Whether you want to be a model or actor, a better entrepreneur or business professional, or you just want to become a better person, personal development is the way. And if you are considering modeling or acting, I honestly believe anyone can do it. There is a market for every look.

After sharing the screen with stars such as Dwayne "The Rock" Johnson on the set of HBO's Ballers, working with directors such as Michael Bay on the set of Transformers, and doing commercials for brands such as Corona, Home Depot, and Jeep to name a few, I have learned a ton on my journey. However, there has been no greater truth revealed than the need to personally grow and develop skills in the respective craft, every day.

I started as a nobody. I didn't know one thing about the entertainment industry nor did I really know anyone who did. Just like anything you want to accomplish, you have to start by educating yourself on the topic. You have to get familiar with the industry language and the business inner workings. You have to understand the process and industry policy. You also should understand what is going to hold you back and what is going to help you succeed.

For me, personal development in this area was a multitude of different endeavors simultaneously. I sought to find a mentor in the entertainment business. I studied professionals who were at the top of their game. I read books about the industry. I networked with professional agents, casting directors, talent managers, and heck, anyone who would talk to me. Becoming a working professional and actually getting paid for your services in any industry requires you to first become a student of the game.

My Journey in the Entertainment Industry

Let me preface this story by saying that the entertainment industry is a beast of a business and though it appears glamorous on TV, the truth is very different. It started when I was 16 and joined a scam agency in Florida. For those that don't know the 'industry', an agency is composed of agents who represent multiple models and actors. Some agencies have a large board of talent ranging from a couple hundred to just a couple of dozen talents in which they represent. This was the type of agency that had a couple hundred and collected a sign-up fee from each new talent. This particular agency hosted "masterclasses" and invited the parents of the talent, and then selected the individuals that they want to represent. This was basically anyone willing to pay the $500 sign-up cost. FYI: Any agent that wants you to pay upfront for anything is *not* legitimate. Do not waste your time or money! That was my rude introduction to the industry and my first time getting ripped off by crooked agents. But, not my last.

After earning a college soccer scholarship, I later moved to Chicago and began Happy Hustlin' the internet for any modeling/acting jobs that I could find in my free time to make some extra cash. I would scavenge Craigslist and submit to dozens of job posts per week. I started doing "test shoots" with photographers to build my portfolio. A test shoot is a photoshoot where the photographer and model trade services rather than a monetary exchange. I was getting more comfortable in front of the camera, but was definitely not there yet. My first paying modeling job was actually found on Craigslist. I still remember the listing title which read, "Looking for Great Male Legs". I was playing college soccer at the time and thought I had a decent shot. I left in the middle of my sophomore English class and snapped some calf pics on my cell phone in the bathroom. Quite awkward. There I was having a photoshoot with my calves when another student walked in. Nonetheless, I did it and submitted the photos. I later found out it was for a Croc's shoot, yes, those same plastic fashionable clogs, and I booked the job! The following week, I was in a studio smiling, profiling, and flexing my calves in a variety of Croc's finest in exchange for $400, which was a pretty decent coin for me at the time. After cashing the check, I remember splurging on beer and Taco Bell for all the college bros.

The funniest part of the job was when I got the actual magazine sent to me. I eagerly tore through the pages searching for my mug only to find out that the whole shoot was from the waist down! Not one picture of my face.

The only way I could even recognize my calf over the others was a scar from a skatepark rollerblading incident and my blondish leg hair.

Talk about my first claim to fame!

Anyway, I slowly paid my dues in the industry thereafter. I began taking acting classes. Then, my improv journey at The Second City in Chicago commenced. I dove all in, committing to completing levels A – E of thier training program. Each letter signifies an 8-week course based on an improv principle. I soaked up the knowledge from each of the talented teachers and learned different comedic tools. Every class was fun and exciting. Although, I didn't fully realize until later on in my career how valuable the lessons were. Being hungry for more improv and training, I volunteered at Second City and waited tables during the main stage and stand-up shows. My goal was to be around the talented performers and watch the shows for free.

HAPPY HUSTLE HACK

Find a way to physically put yourself in an environment conducive to learning and success based on your goals. I knew this was the mecca of improv with former alumni Steve Carrell, Tina Fey, Amy Poehler, Jason Sudeikis, Mike Myers, and Chris Farley, to name a few. I volunteered, hosted, waited tables, etc. during this time. I did whatever I had to do in order to spend more time around Second City. The point being, find a way to soak up knowledge.

Let's fast forward to 2011 when I was studying abroad in Barcelona. This is when it changed from, "Yea, I want to be a model/actor" to "Whoa, I'm actually getting paid for my image!" It snowballed after a random encounter with a Polish girl at an El Corte Engles (their big department store) when buying white pants for an all-white themed, all night rager. She invited me to a super edgy model party on top of the Grand Hotel. Thankfully, I was quite "edgy" myself with a mustache, red rattail (yes, I dyed it), serious mutton chop sideburns, and some double pierced ears, filled with black, fake diamond earrings.

I know, what was I thinking. The party looked like a Corona Light commercial with a DJ spinning poolside, trays of fancy finger foods, individuals rocking hoop earrings down to the navel, parlayed with random eccentric tattoos. It was an interesting setting. It was sponsored by Wrangler International Jeans, not the Brett Favre dad jeans or cowboy dungarees, but rather a more stylish version. I got scouted there by an agent from ICON Barcelona Modeling Agency. The next day I was in my undies taking digitals (raw, unedited pictures) in his office. The following day after that, I was picked up by a guy on a moped out front of my homestay for an undisclosed epic photoshoot.

Here I was hitching on to some random Spaniard on his moped with my rattail flowing in the breeze and no idea where I was headed. We rode to Barceloneta Beach and pulled up to the W Hotel, one of the most prestigious, iconic hotels in the city. I had never been there since I couldn't even afford a one-night stay at the time. I was greeted by the stylist and client. They took me up to the penthouse where they had 4 racks of the nicest clothes I had ever seen in person, let alone worn. There was another male model there who, as it turned out, was quite popular in Spain. I thought for sure I would probably be his door guy or background beotch for the photoshoot. But, as luck would have it, I was the principal talent and he was pouring me tea and holding my doors on camera all day!

I honestly had no clue what I was doing for this first photoshoot. The only reason I can assume they chose me was that I had a different look with my facial hair and 'mohawk-ish' cut. I was also 21 years old and in good shape. Fortunately, they were willing to coach me throughout the process. We shot all day and I changed into at least 8 different outfits. At one point, I was rocking a bowtie worth a 350 Euros and a ridiculously expensive suit with matching red velvet dress shoes. I didn't know what the photos were exactly intended for at the time, but heck, I was just happy to be getting a catered lunch!

My first magazine cover... little lip caterpillar and all.

The shoot wrapped up and I was stoked with the day's work. A couple of months later, I finally found out what the photos were used for. I was walking down the street and passed one of the gay men's stores. A magazine called,

"SHENGAY" sat storefront with my picture on the cover! Yep, a gay mag and my real first claim to fame. They also sold the editorial photos to a magazine called "COOLTURE," which my mug was on the cover of that as well. Quite funny to me now, looking back.

With my newfound experience, I was cast and booked for a Degree deodorant international commercial. I remember they cast me with my mustache and wanted me to shave it when I got to set. Then, production was upset that they made me shave it. Anyway, we were shooting at a large film studio in Barcelona's outskirts. This one paid some big bucks, over 5,000 Euros, just for the buyout alone. This was the most legit set I had been on at the time with 50+ people buzzing around all with important jobs to do. I, on the other hand, was resting my eyes in the corner. Unprofessional, to say the least. I shot my part and was off awaiting my big payday. My agent in Barcelona, Andreu, claimed the money takes 90 days to be paid. Since I was set to be back in the U.S. before then, I was banking on his honesty that he would send my check through the mail. The money never arrived nor did he answer any of my calls, emails, texts, etc. If you see Andreu, let me know. Better yet, kick him in the gonads for your boy. Needless to say, it was a valuable lesson early on in my career.

I did, however, get great pictures for my portfolio and had some amazing experiences while modeling in Spain. When I got back to the states, I convinced a couple of other agents in Chicago to sign me. I continued to build my portfolio by booking a couple of hundred-dollar jobs each month. I was on the grind daily. I self-submitted for gigs and networked with every, and any, industry professional I could find both digitally with cold emails and physically by putting myself in the right rooms.

When I left Chicago to head back to Florida, I had experience in commercial acting, at least a dozen paid photoshoots under my belt, and 3+ years of acting/improv classes. I knew Miami had a strong market and began researching to determine the top 5 agencies. I had just bought a new motorcycle at the time and made my way from Sarasota to Miami to meet with several of those agencies. This is when I ended up getting a serious $1,000 speeding ticket with an additional 100 community service hours after being clocked at 178 mph on "Alligator Alley" like a real knucklehead. This explains the image earlier in this book. This setback made it all the more important to get signed and start making money!

The first agency I knew I wanted to go to was Wilhelmina. This was the top agency in Miami, and in the world for that matter, with locations in over a dozen major cities. I did my research knowing who the director and bookers were and how many guys were on their online model database - A.K.A.: "board." I walked in the door with my motorcycle helmet in one hand and my printed picture portfolio in the other.

Usually, they don't take walk-ins whatsoever. But, I schmoozed the front desk girl to get my book passed back to the bookers. One of the bookers came out, he happened to speak Spanish, and I did my best to charm him with my own recently acquired broken Spanish from living abroad. Then, the director of the men's board came out, leafed through my portfolio, and offered me a 3-year contract! I couldn't believe it. It was a combination of luck, preparation, and good timing. I didn't sign the contract on the spot, but rather told them I had a "couple other meetings" and would get back to them by the end of the week. You know, a little 'hardball'.

This was a massive feat since I'd previously been a "take anything I could get scavenging Craigslist" type of model/actor. And now, here I was being offered a contract by the world's most highly acclaimed talent agency. An interesting and humbling journey, nonetheless. I was reluctant to sign anything for 3 years but proceeded anyway. It didn't end up working out as I presumed or would have liked. But, it was another valuable lesson in the industry. I later moved on to another very sought-after agency, arguably as big as Wilhelmina, called NEXT Models. I continued on to work with other world-renowned agencies and agents, booking amazing lucrative gigs all the while. On your journey, you will build momentum which often stacks success upon success. That's what happened to me. When you are personally developing yourself and your skills consistently, opportunities arise.

Baby face Cary in 3-piece suit action.

The modeling/acting industry can be an ugly business at times. Rejection is ever-present and ample individuals are looking to take advantage of you and your talents. You must be wary upon entering contracts and working with agencies, clients, photographers, and other talents. This lesson, in particular, can be applied to every industry. Know what you are signing, especially contracts. As boring as the legal jargon of contracts can be, read through every word as it is critical to get in the habit of using extreme discretion with your signature. Recognize that if it is not legally in writing, it doesn't mean shit. That handshake deal is only as good as both parties' integrity, so when it is written and signed by both parties, it can be legally enforced.

ACTIONABLE TAKEAWAY

One other thing I've taken away from my journey is that **you must pay your dues. As with anything worth doing, it takes time and effort.** It takes networking. It takes awkward conversations. It takes Happy Hustlin'. You have to be willing to put forth the energy and spend hours honing your craft. Put yourself out there and don't be afraid to fail. Rejection is a part of business and life. It is said that the acting/modeling industry has a 97% unemployment rate. Literally, 9 out of 10 actors/models are NOT working on any given day. That means, at times we must find other means of income. Many turn to freelance promo modeling, brand ambassador work, and event catering. Hustlin' is the name of the game.

I hunted for my own jobs. I researched and dropped into casting director's officesto meet with photographers and clients myself. I would bring cookies and a smile everywhere. Literally, I had multiple trays with handwritten notes ready to be customized to any given professional that I was attempting to network with. And it worked! I would often book the gig and found myself working more regularly thanks to these methods.

HAPPY HUSTLE HACK

Give food and goodies as gifts. People love unexpected treats and will remember them. :) This brash approach works like a charm. I bet it would work for your industry too. To be remembered, stand out and be different! For context, I used to go to over 100 castings per year and book roughly between 15-25 major jobs. Now, the number is far less as my focus shifted to running my other businesses. That means I was getting rejected about 80% of the time! But, I continued to show up time and time again knowing that it only takes one to make it worth it. For instance, one summer I ended up booking 3 SAG (Screen Actors Guild) National Commercials: Home Depot, Corona, and Jeep. These netted me upwards of $20k for each commercial. $60k for technically 3 days of work! So, the hard work can pay off quickly.

You never know exactly who needs you and your services, so you have to keep showing up. The lesson here is to not get discouraged about the previous failures, fam. Persist forward to the next opportunity!

I am very grateful for the ability to act and model professionally. Sometimes on set, I stand in awe asking how I got so lucky to be paid to smile or give "blue-steel" depending on the gig in exotic locations all over the world with some of the most beautiful people on this planet. Blessed, indeed. But, it definitely didn't come easy. It took time, relentless pursuit, and consistent persistency. It took Happy Hustlin' and doing things others wouldn't. If you're willing to work for what you want and can push through the rejection, you can do it too. Just don't take no for an answer and stay steady in your pursuit of growth. Results will follow dedicated effort. Think about what personal development is required for success in your industry and how you can start improving your skills today. Then, get after it!

Although I look sad in this photo, I am actually super happy and grateful that I get paid to do things I enjoy with people I enjoy. A.K.A.: Happy Hustlin'. Steph and I often still get booked to model/act together. This is one of my favorite photos of us by the talented Yasmine Kateb.

EMBARRASSING FUN FACT

I once snuck into a 3-day long personal development conference. I didn't have any money at the time and resorted to fabricating a makeshift badge, dressing in a suit, and waltzing in with confidence. I sat in the front row soaking up knowledge before being asked for my credentials and eventually publicly getting the boot at the end of day 2. #worthit

POWERFUL RESOURCES

Books:
The Compound Effect by Darren Hardy
The ONE Thing by Gary Keller

Podcasts:
The School of Greatness with Lewis Howes
Impact Theory with Tom Bilyeu
The Happy Hustle with Cary Jack, Episode 3, 24, 180, 182

Movie:
The Pursuit of Happyness with Will Smith

ALIGNMENT 8
PASSIONATE HOBBIES

"FUN IS A NON-NEGOTIABLE"
– CARY JACK

Do Fun Things You Like. Regularly Enjoy Hobbies

Alright you Happy Hustler, first let me say that you are crushing it! You are well on your way to Happy Hustlin' a life you truly love. One full of blissful balance. Keep reading. Keep going. Keep implementing!

This Alignment is personally one of my favorites! It is all about enjoying the hobbies you love to do! Yes, I am encouraging you to do things that have no monetary reward, even if you have to pay for them. What is it all for if you're not having fun and enjoying yourself along the journey, right?

Depending on where you ranked yourself (1-5) in this Alignment, listen up! I find many entrepreneurs and busy professionals who often don't make time for themselves or their hobbies. It's time to identify what non-work-related activities you love to do and actually schedule them into your weekly routine. Whether it's an oil painting, swing dancing, playing pick-up basketball, playing cards, swimming, or knitting, this is where you give yourself permission to do the thing and do it regularly!

At a minimum, I find two hobbies per week to be the necessary frequency for me to feel balanced.

Some of the hobbies that I enjoy doing are Krav Maga: Israeli Self-Defense Survival System, playing competitive soccer, fly fishing, reading, and dancing. When I include these hobbies into my week, I am happier and my life is more fulfilling because of it.

I usually schedule each item at least once per week depending on when each activity takes place. For instance, I usually play in a competitive men's soccer league every Sunday morning, Steph and I take dance classes every Wednesday, and Krav Maga is every Tuesday and Thursday evening. Fishing is whenever I can fit it in, either sunrise or sunset as that is the best time to fish. So, choose your activity and then schedule the time in which you will do it.

Start first by identifying:

- **What are your top 3 favorite hobbies?** Think about what you really enjoy doing.
- **When will you do each of those hobbies this week?** Find time. Some hobbies may require others/instructors/etc. You may have to move your schedule to fit when the hobby is being offered.
- **Who do you need to call/text/email to schedule your hobby?** Do that now. Seriously, stop reading and take action on this.

Don't breeze over these questions. Answer them before continuing and put them into your calendar NOW. This book was created to actually help you Happy Hustle, not just talk about it. But, you gotta take action. I can show you the door to the promised land and give you the key. But, ultimately it is you who must open it and go in!

Diversification

I highly recommend not just doing the hobbies you have always done. Try adding in a new one to your life about every 3-6 months. For instance, I am starting to get my pilot's license and looking forward to the freedom that comes with piloting my own plane. This way, life will never get boring and you can continue to learn and develop new skills!

Diversification is not only beneficial for your financial investment portfolio, my friend, but it is also beneficial for your hobby portfolio. What are you curious about? What skill or activity have you seen in the movies or online, and thought to yourself, "Man, I want to try that!" Maybe it's kite-boarding, martial arts, or board games. Who knows what it is for you. The point is, expand yourself and your skillset by doing new things regularly!

Nerdy point: Developing new skills helps develop neuroplasticity in the brain and actually creates new brain connections. It's not only good for your routine, it's good for your brain to switch it up!

Think about and answer the following questions. Write them in your handy journal, notepad, or wherever you've been taking notes throughout this book.

- *What is a new activity or hobby you have been wanting to do?*
- *When will you do it?* I want you to put down a clear date in the next 6 months.
- *What is needed in order to begin this activity or hobby?* Acquire the resources and get it done!

Priorities

To ensure that you are following through with your passionate hobbies, add them to your calendar and treat them with the same priority level as you would a work meeting. This is an important key point that I want to elaborate. This means your Zoom business meeting gets the same priority as your pick up basketball game and the same goes for your date night with your significant other! All of them get equal priority on your calendar to ensure they get done.

This is a meeting for yourself and must be valued. Without regularly doing these things that you love, your life will become out of balance. Don't let yourself off the hook. It's sometimes easy to cancel on ourselves. Don't do it. Be disciplined enough to prioritize the things that you love to do, not just the things you 'have to do'. If you want to be a Happy Hustler, this is an absolute must. Do fun things and enjoy Passionate Hobbies regularly! You earned it!

HAPPY HUSTLER SPOTLIGHT

Garrett Gravesen

I want to spotlight my Happy Hustlin' friend Garrett Gravesen. He is a world traveler, entrepreneur, author, and storyteller. He definitely knows how to have fun and implement passionate hobbies into his life! Garrett has traveled to all 7 continents and every country in the worlD. Yes, all 195. That is quite the feat since less than 300 people out of 7+ billion have done it! And he's done so wearing a tuxedo to just about all of them. This includes Antarctica, Machu Picchu, the Great Wall of China, and the middle of Afghanistan among numerous other amazing places.

I met Garrett at a Brand Builders Group event and we instantly hit it off. I had him on the Happy Hustle Podcast: Episode #31. I invite you to listen to it if you fancy. Garrett is so charismatic and drops non-stop value bombs in the form of captivating stories. You are going to love this episode!

He authored the best-selling book *10 Seconds of Insane Courage* (great read). He was recently named one of the "Ten Outstanding Young People of the World". Garrett also co-founded a leadership consulting firm ADDO Worldwide and the ADDO Institute.

Garrett is a proud alumnus of Harvard Business School and the University of Georgia, where he became the youngest student body president in school history.

Before attending Harvard, Garrett did investment banking for Merrill Lynch & CO in Hong Kong and worked at an AIDS orphanage in Africa for a year.

Garrett co-founded H.E.R.O. for Children, the largest pediatric AIDS organization in Georgia, and the Global LEAD Program. They galvanized over 10,000 next-generation leaders' in-service programs in the United States, Africa, and Europe. He speaks at conferences and companies about innovation, storytelling, and "10 Seconds of Insane Courage." But most of all, he knows how to incorporate his passionate hobby of traveling into his life and we can all learn from that!

Garrett in his tux at the bottom of Angel Falls in Venezuela. My man G is living his best life and Happy Hustlin' around the world.

STORY TIME: THE BEST EDUCATION YOU CAN GET IN THE WORLD

If I haven't stressed it enough already, traveling is literally one of the greatest things you can do on this earth. Traveling is one of my go-to Happy Hustlin' hobbies. Meeting new people, learning different languages, experiencing foreign cultures, eating delicious and often odd foods. These all add up to unforgettable experiences which often teach us lessons.

Knowledge acquired through experience is rarely disregarded or forgotten. Personally, I have learned many things from traveling that will stick with me for the rest of my life. Things like keeping my wallet in my front pocket to better avoid pickpockets in Barcelona or always asking the locals about the best places to eat. That's how I found epically delicious pho in Vietnam and got up early to visit historic monuments and sites to beat the lines, which I learned at Foz De Acquzu (the waterfalls) on the Argentine/Brazilian border.

My bro Sammy & I at Angkor Wat in Cambodia, aka one of the 7 Wonders of the World.

Knowing north, south, east, and west in a country's native language helps tremendously when navigating. This was especially necessary in Bangkok. Another lesson learned is testing your comfort zone. I usually like to push the boundaries which tends to get me and my travel compadres wrapped up in some hairy situations.

One time, my brother and I got on the back of two mopeds in Argentina, illegally crossed the border, and didn't stop to show proper documentation at the border patrol booths to Paraguay. Apparently, it's common there. Grant's moped driver might as well have been a former Nascar racer. I was certain that I was going to witness his death at the hands of this 5-foot nothing Paraguayan who nearly collided head-on with a semi-truck before just barely swerving out of the way. But that wasn't all. Even after we got off the mopeds, we were still in extreme danger as they dropped us off in one of the biggest slums in the border city of

Asunción. We were the only gringos in sight and definitely a target. We were approached by sex workers, gang members, heroin addicts, and dealers before finally being told to essentially run in Español by an older woman, and angel, with her daughter. I guess the locals were planning an attack! We did just that. We booked it out of there and made it to the border where the military police escorted us back to Argentina. That time, our comfort zone was stretched for sure. The lesson is to be smart when pushing the limits.

Know that with traveling comes opportunity and responsibility. You often have an opportunity to push yourself to break internal barriers and it is your responsibility to embrace the experience at hand, live in the moment, and go for it. Traveling often dictates a shrunken 'comfort zone' as many experiences will be all-new and foreign. Therefore, you have the opportunity to grow almost every day just by stepping outside and doing things you've never done. Just remain conscious of your surroundings and make smart choices when pushing your personal boundaries. Get out there and travel. Enjoy some passionate hobbies along the way! Book your next trip. Plan, prepare, and execute. Barring there are no travel bans due to a pandemic at the time of this writing, the time is now. You won't regret it!

ACTIONABLE TAKEAWAY

Whether you choose to make traveling your passionate hobby or biking, fishing, painting, dancing, whatever it is for you, just do it regularly. **Feed your soul with fun. Life is too short to postpone your passions.** Balance the things you need to do with the things you want to do. Once again, balance equals happiness. Please, please, please make sure you incorporate passionate hobbies into your schedule. Do the things you love with the people you care about and do them frequently!

EMBARRASSING FUN FACT

I once attempted to join the mile-high club with a beautiful stranger sitting in 8E. I boldly wrote on a piece of paper, "You're beautiful. The names JC. Meet me in the bathroom at 6:30 PM ;)" JC is my alter ego. Within five minutes of dropping the note and before taking off, her entire row and surrounding 3 rows began turning around and looking at me as I sat in the last aisle seat... right next to the bathroom. What started as our little secret, I quickly turned out to be the laughing stock of the plane. 6:30 PM came around and guess who came walking down the aisle? The nameless beauty... followed closely by her stern-faced, military-looking general of a father.

She walked past with a little smirk and then entered the bathroom. Her father was not so coy as he crouched down 2 inches from my face and said, "You got a lot of fucking nuts kid. You know that guy you reached over to hand your forward proposal to was her fiancé. We're on the way to her destination wedding, pal. The three rows around her are filled with the family."

My heart sank. He then grabbed me by my thigh with his iron grip and pushed himself up, all the while, staring directly into my eyes. He then proceeded back to his seat after his daughter, who I then claimed to be my brunette beauty, exited the bathroom.

The embarrassment did not stop there and boy does this story take a turn for the worse. As we hit some turbulent weather forcing us to make an emergency landing, we sat on the tarmac for over two hours before having to ultimately exit the plane. Do you know how many times each family member went to the bathroom? A lot. Talk about awkward conversations over and over again. What makes things even worse is due to the extreme weather, we actually had to stay the night in the same hotel and share the same plane the next morning! Once again, the embarrassment dragged on and on for what felt like an eternity. By the end of it, I was legit on a first name basis with her and every single one of her family members. And yes, including her fiancé who was actually pretty cool. I definitely know how to laugh at myself and this was just one of those times where I had to do just that. Talk about an epic failure. That day still goes down in history as one of the most embarrassing moments of my life. However, I'll have you know, my fiancé and I are now a proud members of the club.

POWERFUL RESOURCES

Books:
The Peaceful Warrior by Dan Millan *(This book changed my life. I even have "Peaceful" & "Warrior" tattooed on my inner biceps. 100% worth the read.)*
The Alchemist by Paulo Coehlo

Podcasts:
Joe Rogan Podcast

Online Resource:
OIS Krav Maga with World-Renowned Instructor Phillip Glikman

Author's Note: When people ask me which of the martial arts to practice first, I always recommend Krav Maga. It is the most lethal, practical, and efficient of all the many martial arts that I have trained. And also, my favorite.

ALIGNMENT 9
IMPACTFUL WORK

"YOUR WORK IS GOING TO FILL A LARGE PART OF YOUR LIFE, AND THE ONLY WAY TO BE TRULY SATISFIED IS TO DO WHAT YOU BELIEVE IS GREAT WORK. AND THE ONLY WAY TO DO GREAT WORK IS TO LOVE WHAT YOU DO. IF YOU HAVEN'T FOUND IT YET, KEEP LOOKING. DON'T SETTLE. AS WITH ALL MATTERS OF THE HEART, YOU'LL KNOW WHEN YOU FIND IT."
– STEVE JOBS

If You Want It, Use The Happy Hustle Dote To Go Get It

I was rockin' a $3000 Prada suit, leopard Tom Ford loafers (both of which I got for pennies thanks to a modeling gig), and swanky Persol sunglasses on my way to an investor meeting in Manhattan with my brother Grant. We were "faking it until we made it." We had lined up multiple potential VCs for our tech start-up Feedbakr and were looking to solidify a 7-figure funding deal. We were indeed hustlin', working 100+ hour weeks. But, we were not happy.

Our days consisted of getting up every day before the sun for a workout, hopping on the grimy morning 30-minute subway ride, walking blocks in uncomfortable dumb fancy shoes, grindin' in our entrepreneurial co-working space, a quick lunch meeting break, heading back to the office to continue the beta app build-out, evening cocktails at a networking meet-up, a 30+ minute subway ride home, and getting to bed just before midnight only to get up and do it all over again the next day. At the time, my brother and I were actually sharing a king-sized bed in a shithole apartment in the Sunnyside Queens neighborhood and ballin' on a budget, to say the least. Let me tell ya, it was far from a balanced, beautiful life. It wasn't until we actually landed the 7-figure funding deal and partnerships with IBM and Microsoft that I realized, "Oh shit, we're hustlin' but not happy". Something had to change.

Acknowledge The Current Situation

The first step in creating a purposeful business or career is acknowledging your current situation and where you are. Think about where you ranked yourself in this Alignment (1-5). Are you working a job you dislike or even hate? Do you wake up and dread going to the office? Is there a conflict with your boss or co-workers? If you could make money doing something else, what would you actually want to be getting up and doing with your time? You must truly identify where you are in terms of your impactful work, or lack thereof. Ask yourself what you actually want to be doing.

See, before finalizing the funding deal and inking the paperwork to solidify the offer and partnerships, we had a heart-to-heart conversation. We were both exhausted and burned the F out. Tears streamed from our eyes as we sat across from one another at the watermarked stained table in the dump of a kitchen we called home. In that moment, we decided it was best for us and the business to pivot. More on this decision in the upcoming Story Time...

Grant and I on the grind at Microsoft offices in NYC.

Make a Game Plan

After we acknowledged that we were feeling unhappy and unfulfilled, it was time to get crystal clear on what my brother and I really wanted. What was our true vision for our lives? What did we wish to create? What was God's plan for us? If you believe in that sort of thing.

I recommend making a game plan as to how you are going to exit your current career if it is not fulfilling. If you are not happy with your reality, you have the power to change it. You have the ability to be brave and make a different choice. Say no to what you don't want and *hell yes* to what you do. You can Happy Hustle a new future with a purposeful career and it starts right now.

3 Questions to Impactful Work

As my friends at Brand Builders Group teach as a part of their curriculum, start by asking yourself these 3 questions.

- *WHAT problem do you feel called to solve?*
- *WHO do you feel called to solve that problem for?*
- *And what is YOUR uniqueness and how can you exploit it in the service of others?*

The What

"Business is solving problems at a profit", like my friend Wade Lightheart says. He is the co-founder of the multi-million-dollar company Bioptimizers. Check out episode #109 on The Happy Hustle Podcast to listen to the awesome interview. Don't overcomplicate it. Just think, what problem do you actually want to solve? What cause speaks to you personally? How could you combine your skills and knowledge to create a solution? Try to distill the problem that you solve into ONE word. That type of specificity will ensure the clarity that is necessary for success. For me, the one-word problem that I solve is imbalance. Hence, why I wrote this book to help you avoid burnout and achieve blissful balance. Think what that one word could be for you.

If you're stuck here, ponder what you have overcome that gives you the right to solve that problem for people and the planet. Most often, "Our mess becomes our message" as Nicholas Bayerle says. Check out episode #13 on The Happy

Hustle Podcast to see the awesome interview I did with him. Decide what problem that is and how you can be the one to solve it! In one word... clarity!

The Who

Next, decide who exactly you want to solve the problem for. This is a crucial part of actually achieving fulfillment and happiness from your work. If you solve problems for people that you don't like or love to be around, then you will find yourself dreading the act of helping them! Choose to solve the problem for a targeted niché of the population that you actually want to serve and associate yourself with. For me, I love solving the problem of imbalance for purpose-driven entrepreneurs. I am a purpose-driven entrepreneur, hence why I like helping others on a similar mission! Oftentimes, we like solving problems for those who are in our old shoes or where we were.

Once you can identify the target niché you want to solve the problem for, go a mile deep and an inch wide. Most companies and entrepreneurs say, "I can help everyone. Buy my stuff". They go a mile wide and an inch deep, then wonder why their marketing doesn't land. Happy Hustlers, A.K.A: you, instead spend the time to find out everything about your perfect target avatar. You go a mile deep. They deep dive demographics like age, sex, location, marital status, income, etc. and psychographics like personality traits, lifestyle choices, opinions, beliefs, morals, interests, etc. When you can get to know your perfect target avatar at this level of detail, you can then cut through the noisy ass marketplace that is out there and speak directly to them with your message. With this clarity, instead of 'pushing' marketing content, you will be 'pulling' opportunity seekers into your world. Once you have your perfect avatar's attention, you can add value to them and nurture a relationship. The key point here is to actually nurture the relationship. Don't just go right for the sale before adding sufficient value and building trust. When the time is right you can present them your product or service to solve their problem. Voilà! You're making money solving a problem you care about for people you care about, thus, creating impactful work. Boom shakalaka. My toes are wiggling uncontrollably as I write this fire-side in my red plaid jammies from pure excitement for you to heed the above insights and infuse more meaning into your work! You know it's good when the toe-wiggles come on.

Uniqueness

Now, the next level to crushing purposeful, impactful work is exploiting your uniqueness in the service of others. You may be thinking, "But Cary, I don't know what the heck my uniqueness is?" Here's a quick way to figure it out. Ask your 10 closest relationships in your life, "What attribute of yours do they appreciate the most?" Then write down each response and note the most common, similar answers. If you don't want to reach out to others in your inner circle, then write down:

- *5 things that make you feel authentically you.*
- *5 things you feel you are uniquely good at.*

Cross-reference the list and pick out the top 1 from each list to combine into your uniqueness to help you serve your perfect target avatar!

Your Hustlin' Why

I see Hustlin' as busting your ass and working hard, although many use the word differently. When I have been discussing Hustlin' in this book, I use it with the definition of doing whatever it takes to get what you want. Staying up late, waking up early, making cold calls, showing up without a meeting, getting rejected over and over again but still continuing anyway. This is Hustlin' to me. Hustlin' usually only occurs when you want something bad enough to do whatever it takes to get it. When you are willing to put in the sweat equity. When time spent doesn't matter, only getting results do.

To hustle harder than ever before, you have to find your why deep within yourself. What is the purpose behind your work? Why are you doing it? Why do you want what you want? This is your fuel. When you are feeling down, rejected, or discouraged, the why is what will lift you up to keep pushing. The thought of status and material things typically aren't strong enough for you to persevere in the toughest of times. Your why needs to be emotionally charged. For me, my mom is sick. Due to her illness, as a kid, we moved 24 times before I was 18-years old. I watched her suffer for years. Struggling with her health. I want so badly to build her a healthy, toxin-free home, supply her with top-notch items (supplements, equipment, testing, etc), and give her the world's best professional care to heal. It fuels me every day. The pain from her experience (along with my own relentless drive) pushes me to do whatever it takes. When you find a reason worth pursuing, it will change everything. Your why may change over time. That's ok. Just make sure to have one so strong it fuels you past the inevitable adversity. So get clear on your why today.

The Happy Hustle-Dote Formula

There is a formula to hustlin' that I created and utilize every day. It's a formula that has been proven and tested. When followed and implemented, it has the power to achieve desires you only ever dreamed of.

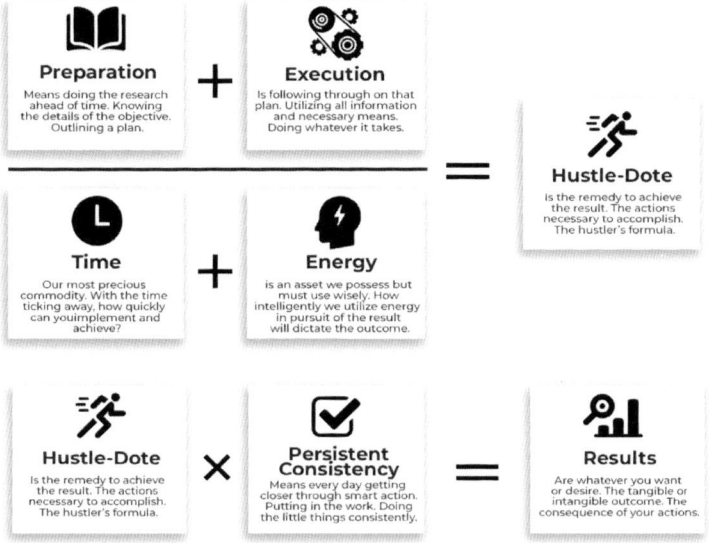

Preparation means doing the research ahead of time. Knowing the details of the objective. Outlining a plan.

Execution is following through on that plan. Utilizing all information and necessary means. Doing whatever it takes.

Time is our most precious commodity. With the time ticking away, how quickly can you implement and achieve?

Energy is an asset we possess but must use wisely. How intelligently we utilize energy in pursuit of the result will dictate the outcome.

Happy Hustle-Dote is the remedy to achieve the result. The actions are necessary to accomplish. The Happy Hustler's formula to success.

Persistent Consistency means every day getting closer through smart action. Putting in the work. Doing the little things consistently.

Results are whatever you want or desire. The tangible or intangible outcome. The consequence of your actions.

You can use this Happy Hustle-dote to achieve everything you want in this life and more. This Happy Hustle-Dote used in conjunction with a clear vision will heed the desired results in your life. Don't take this shit lightly. This is the golden ticket to your chocolate factory boys and girls. If you got a sweet tooth for a sweet life, use the Happy Hustle-Dote to satisfy that craving and Happy Hustle your dream reality!

So, there you have it. Three (3) questions for you to answer and the Happy Hustle Dote to help you achieve purposeful work in your life today! If you already feel purpose in your work, amazing! Use these questions to dive deeper and become even more clear so you can help even more people. The world needs your message. Take action. Don't sacrifice your time doing meaningless work any longer. The time is now for you to combine your passion and purpose into Impactful Work that actually makes a positive difference in the world. Yee yeeiii!

HAPPY HUSTLER SPOTLIGHT

John Lee Dumas

John Lee Dumas is an Army veteran, founder, and host of the award-winning podcast, Entrepreneurs On Fire. With over 100 million listens of his 3000+ episodes, JLD has turned Entrepreneurs On Fire into a media empire that generates over a million listens every month and 7-figures of net annual revenue 8 years in a row. His first traditionally published book, *The Common Path to Uncommon Success* is the modern-day version of *Think and Grow Rich* with a revolutionary 17-step roadmap to financial freedom and fulfillment. JLD is for sure a Happy Hustler and lives in a beautiful beach home in Puerto Rico (which saves him millions in taxes). He interviews with so much spunky energy and knows how to extract usable value that actually teaches his audience. He even started out by releasing daily podcast episodes, which at the time, no one was doing that type of frequency, a true pioneer in the industry.

I personally got the chance to connect with JLD and have since built an amazing friendship. He even gave me a testimonial quote for this very book (check out the back cover). It all started when I realized he was going to be in South Florida speaking at an event. I bought tickets for my girlfriend at the time (now fiance') and me to attend and then sent him an email. The headline of the email read, "While you're in Florida next month, want to come to Biohack with some bros?!" Knowing he is serious about optimizing his health, I then outlined all the value included in our "Decade in a Day," a high-ticket biohacking immersion experience, a day dedicated personally to you and your health, where we condensed a decade worth of biohacking, biological age-reversal, and wellness strategies into one-day, all customized based on your current health status and goals. At the time, we sold these for $7,500 a day but offered them to JLD for FREE, knowing the value of fostering a relationship. We offered him rides, a place to stay, food, workouts, biohacks, the whole she-bang. To my surprise, he responded within an hour with "FUCK yes." I legit laughed out loud. He was super pumped and as were we.

It was now the time of the event and JLD crushed his speech and even closed I think over 200k from the room after selling access to his Podcasters Paradise. He greeted the crowd of event attendees who were itching for a picture and advice. He then hopped in my truck and we headed for Delray Beach. Here I was driving one of my entrepreneurial idols to come to spend the night, all because I took a chance, reached out, and offered massive value to something I knew he was interested in.

We got to Biohacking HQ and my biz partner at the time Anthony, JLD and I then went for a run, got delicious takeout, and stayed up late talking like schoolboys at a sleepover. We woke up the next day and gave him the best possible "Decade in a Day" experience. We did biohacks of all kinds – supplement workshops, reviewed his blood work/labs, breathwork, a float tank session, and gave him what he deemed "the best work out of his life." I mean we pushed him to the max and he beasted through it, especially on the battle ropes! We then went out for a fancy oyster and seafood dinner downtown and the day ended with an amazing conversation between JLD and I as I dropped him off at the airport. It was an amazing experience for all of us.

JLD utilizes systems and discipline to accomplish anything he sets his mind to. He has created purposeful work that truly impacts millions of entrepreneurs' lives all over the world. His content, courses, books, videos, podcasts, and messages inspire and educate and he is an example of what is possible when you stay consistent and committed. He is a Happy Hustler through and through. I am grateful for him and the positive impact he has had on my entrepreneurial journey. Check out more about him and his award-winning podcast (and listen to the episode I was featured on by typing Cary Jack in the search) at www.eofire.com

JLD and I after the float tanks...

STORY TIME: FROM NYC BURNOUT TO PURPOSEFUL WORK

Here's a quick story I wanted to share in regards to the Happy Hustle-Dote in action. As mentioned earlier, my brother and I had a tech startup in New York City in 2015 called Feedbakr. It essentially was a platform that quantified human feedback using an algorithm we created. Sparing you too many details, our goal was to help people grow by providing them with what they didn't know about their performance, essentially giving them feedback after meetings and interviews and auditions by the people who were making the decisions. We got an office at an incubator in downtown Manhattan. We went to every meet-up and tech community event we could find. We wore suits every day, even though it was only us in the office in an effort to "dress the tech founders part". We solicited mentors. We pounded the pavement in search of developers. We reached out to big data partners. We pitched every chance we got. Whether in the elevator to a businessman or to a janitor sweeping the floors, we ate, slept, and breathed Feedbakr. We had developed a beta version and had a handful of users but were seeking seed investment to build out the full app platform.

We went to a code developers' session at Microsoft that put us in a room we had no business being in. We basically had no clue what they were talking about in the meeting but nodded our heads throughout like we did. We actually were there to poach coders and gain connections. We stayed after that meet-up and discussed the BizSpark program with the Microsoft liaison. It was a very informative meeting, and we left with a plan of attack to apply.

The next day we went to a talk at Spotify with a panel of distinguished tech evangelists. One of the panelists was an executive at IBM. We, of course, pitched him on our business and he seemed interested. He actually set us up a meeting at IBM with his whole team later that week to hear more. IBM offered at the time a Global Entrepreneurship Program, which parleys into seed investment and tech support. This was a massive meeting for us.

With admission to this program, everything could change and we knew it. On the days leading up to the meeting, we studied and researched nearly everything ever published about IBM. We put in the time and energy to become fully prepared.

When it came time to execute, we were confident and collected, but to be completely transparent, we were also a little intimidated walking into the 100-something floor conference room in downtown Manhattan with a mahogany table and room full of IBM executives in full business mode. We marched into the meeting wearing our finest suits, slide deck ready, print outs with our financial projections and business plan summarized in hand, ready to crush it.

The meeting didn't go as planned. We anticipated the IBM executives would be grilling us on our business but what happened was actually the reverse. We led with the fact that we were at Microsoft earlier that week discussing the BizSpark program (essentially their biggest competitor) and of course we left out that we didn't have a legit offer to join but rather just dropped in on a meet-up. With this status shift, we ended up asking them the questions, asking them why they think we should join their program and how IBM could best serve us! They pitched us so hard. It was quite hilarious in hindsight. Almost a cliché compound by-product of "fake it till you make it" mixed with "knowledge is power." We left that meeting not only with an offer to join the program but also with a massive funding offer.

The moral of this story is that by using the Happy Hustle-Dote and persistent consistency, we found our way to the right room with powerful people that would catalyze our business to a new level. And you can do the same, whatever that looks like for you and your business.

Prepare by formulating a workable plan. Put the time and energy into arming yourself with the necessary knowledge to work that plan. Execute the plan, despite inevitable adversity, do the "thing" that you set out to do. That is the Happy Hustle-Dote. Then continue to use the Happy Hustle-Dote with persistent consistency, every day, anyway. Do this until you get the desired result(s). Then, once you achieve your result, start the process all over again with another goal! I know I make it seem so simple, right. Well, the truth is that the process itself isn't complicated. Doing each step, however, does require discipline and determination. All Happy Hustlin' does. This leads to an important point: *If it is a result worth desiring, find or create the discipline within yourself to commit to the process. And become absolutely determined to accomplish the result.*

Remember, you choose what you want to become. You choose how much you're willing to hustle. You also choose how purposeful that hustle is to you

– so choose wisely. Trust in the process and allow the Happy Hustle-Dote to guide the way. You can achieve it. Believe it, act it, dress it, talk it, be it, do it.

Now let me finish off this Story Time by reminding you of what happened. We said no to the massive funding deal and to both of these entrepreneurial start-up programs as we were burnt the F out. As mentioned earlier in this chapter, we realized that after working our asses off for six months in NYC (and a year prior), we were absolutely spent. Ultimately, when it came down to accepting the 7-figure VC funding deal that came with a 5-year commitment clause (rightfully so, if someone's going to give you that much money, they want to make sure you're in it to win it), we just knew we couldn't take the money. It would have most definitely been the catalyst for our start up becoming a viable mainstream business, hiring a real team, and making big-time money.

Grant & I on that NYC hustle.

However, we also knew that the deal was stuck in quicksand. We would be trapped for at least the next 5 years in the business, slowly sinking into unsatisfying sorrow and that gave us massive anxiety. So we had to listen to our soul's cry and bail. What is your soul crying for?

We also realized that what we were doing was not really aligned with our true calling nor on purpose. We wanted to make a positive impact on the planet but we understood that it was in a different form. So, we made an extremely difficult decision to fold the business, say no to the funding deal and partnerships, and move on in a different direction. My brother and I left New York and went our separate ways, him searching for meaning and purpose elsewhere in the form of a Master's degree at the University of Florida, and me traveling overseas to live in Bangkok, Thailand for 10 months.

It was in Thailand that I realized there was a better way to actually enjoy the journey and infuse meaning into my work. A way to put the Happy in my everyday Hustle. A way to make money and an impact doing something I actually enjoy! And so, The Happy Hustle was born. My goal in sharing this story is to show you that even if you happen to be hustlin' for the wrong reasons currently, or are misaligned with unfulfilling work, it is not too late to to make a change and create purposeful work. If this resonates with you, and you yearn for more fulfillment from your work, allow this to be your wake up call. Ask yourself the 3 questions from above and get on that Impactful Work bandwagon!

ACTIONABLE TAKEAWAY

We are all on a mission for meaning. **Don't waste another moment sacrificing your soul doing work you despise. Answer your calling. Create the Impactful Work in your life that you crave.** You can make money doing what you love. But you must earn that right by doing the work. Answer the above 3 questions. Get crystal clear on your vision. And use the Happy-Hustle Dote to achieve it! You got this baby!

EMBARRASSING FUN FACT

One of the Happy Hustle tactics I have used regularly throughout my journey up the ranks is exploiting free trials and the system behind them. If you are not aware, many businesses and companies give out free trials. For example, WeWork. WeWork is an amazing collaborative workspace for hip, outgoing, entrepreneurs and business people alike. At the time of this writing, WeWork offers free tours & trial days at all of their buildings. They have buildings all over the world, usually multiple in nearly every major city. While my brother and I were getting our hustle on during the growth stages of our first 3 start-ups, we used to find free office space all over the cities we were in. The best part was the network effect. Instead of having the boring, awkward watercooler talk, we would make a point to engage with as many coworkers as possible with probing questions, then listen and learn.

These incubators and collaborative offices usually attract some cool companies with innovative entrepreneurs... and we created the opportunity to rub elbows with as many as possible. We would go to incubators, like WeWork, do a tour of the facility, act very interested in signing up for membership/office space, and then request a trial day. Even when we were just visiting cities, many times instead of working out of an often distracting, busy coffee shop, we would find incubators, request a tour, and then a trial work day, failing to mention our transient status.

We have probably repeated this process in at least a dozen different cities at a ton of incubator workspaces. We would even schedule full-on meetings with potential partners/clients/employees at the incubators that we have never been to.

As mentioned, many times these incubators have inspiring entrepreneurs working there, who are actually paying members. We often would plan our tours around the incubator event schedules. Therefore, we could get some work in then get our networking on. Usually, the events are catered with food and drinks… it's hard to quantify how many free meals we got this way. So that's how we would exploit the "free-trial system" for office spaces in particular.

Also, many businesses will offer free trials even without having the policy to do so, you just have to ask. A Happy Hustler always asks. A Happy Hustler always finds a way… And for the record, I have since paid for a full-on WeWork membership. ;)

POWERFUL RESOURCES

Books:
DotCom Secrets by Russell Brunson
Extreme Ownership by Jocko Wilinik & Leif Babin
The Common Path to Uncommon Success by John Lee Dumas

Podcasts:
The Influential Person Brand Podcast with Rory & AJ Vaden
Impact Theory with Tom Bilyeu
The Ed Mylett Show
Entrepreneurs on Fire with JLD

Movie:
Steve Jobs
The Founder

ALIGNMENT 10
NATURE CONNECTION

"HOW YOU CLIMB A MOUNTAIN IS MORE IMPORTANT THAN REACHING THE TOP."
- YVON CHOUINARD

Disconnect To Connect Our Beautiful Planet Earth

WOW, you are crushing it! You made it to Alignment 10, Nature Connection! The N in the S.O.U.L.M.A.P.P.I.N.™ system. You should be proud of yourself. Many people start books, but most don't finish them. You are well on your way to Happy Hustlin' that life full of blissful balance. Keep going!

One of the Alignments of a Happy Hustler that I believe is missing most in this modern-day life is our visceral connection to nature. We get so caught up in our J O B and routines that we commute to and from our obligations and forget to stop and smell (or even notice) the flowers, trees, or nature on the way. It's like we're tunnel-visioned and completely lacking our primal spirit of connection to Pachamama ("Earth Mother" in Inca mythology). Where did you rank yourself in Nature Connection (1-5)? If you're low in this Alignment, let's prioritize change accordingly.

As we continue to develop as a society, we continue to destroy more natural land to make room for commercial buildings and residential housing. Now I'm not one for halting innovation, however I do believe we must restore the sacred balance between human beings and the natural world. Heck, I honestly feel that is one of the reasons I have been put on this Earth: to help restore BALANCE amongst the people and the planet.

So, here's a real mind-blower, you ready? In order to be more balanced and connected with nature, you guessed it, you have to actually leave your house and actually get outside! I know – crazy, right?

Like seriously people, we're living like zoo animals (which is super sad). We're caged in our homes and apartments, then transition in our cage on wheels to then arrive in our high-rise office cage with a view. If we're lucky, we may get in a quick run outside or a walk in the park but collectively, usually no more than an hour outdoors. So, I ask, do you want to increase your happiness? Good, then get outside more and tune into nature. Get barefoot and walk on the grass. Take a dip in a natural body of water (not a pool). Exercise by going on a hike in a park instead of doing the elliptical at the indoor caged gym. It's time to get back to our roots by re-becoming the wild human animals we are inside.

Protect our Planet

At the current rate, we will not have much nature left to enjoy if we don't start protecting our planet. We have been destroying our natural resources and ecosystems at a tragically shocking rate. We continue to drill pristine wilderness for oil and natural gas. We chop down majestic forests in the name of paper products and the big timber industry. We mine the depths of the soil for unrenewable coal and plutonium. We steal our natural spring water and bottle it up in poisonous plastic containers. We pillage our farmlands in the name of factory farming and industrial agriculture.

Most of our food sources are often genetically modified and are contaminated with toxic pesticides. All of these practices are having a detrimental effect on the health of our planet. We have been living completely unsustainably and it is time we make a change.

We must Happy Hustle for our environment and protect Pacha Mama (Mother Earth), not only for ourselves but for our children and their children. We must implement regenerative eco-practices that are sustainable. We are at the tipping point and scientists predict that if we don't make a massive shift in the next 10 years the damages will be irreversible. If you want to know more about what I'm doing on this matter and how you can help, learn more at caryjack.com/eco-in.

Be an Eco-Warrior

Now I didn't mean to get all doom and gloom on ya there, but it is the truth. We are being greedy AF. Mainly, the major corporations in each particular industry (big oil, gas, logging, agriculture, power, mining, telecommunications, plastic, pharma, etc.).

These large companies are exploiting our Earth for their personal gain with zero remorse and close to no regulations. If we want to stop them before it is too late, we need to come together and speak up!

Become an eco-warrior and advocate for the good of the planet. Don't support companies that utilize unsustainable business practices. Vote every day with your dollar. Only support ethical businesses that focus on the Triple Bottom Line - People, Planet, and Profits. They are out there. Look specifically to support B-Corporations. It may be a little less convenient than buying on Amazon, but spend the extra 5 minutes online properly researching and vetting the companies you buy from. It may even cost you a couple of extra bucks to purchase eco-friendly dish soap or laundry detergent but I promise you, it will collectively make a difference. And you will most likely sleep better knowing you are not contributing to the problem but rather the solution. Here are some simple yet important steps:

- *Bring your own reusable bags to the grocery*
- *Use a reusable water bottle*
- *Support B-Corporations (and buy their products instead of the alternatives)*
- *Bring your own reusable straws & cutlery*
- *Be conscious of your water and electricity usage*
- *Buy local fruits and veggies to support your farmers*
- *Refuse, Reduce, Reuse, Recycle (yes, in that order)*
- *Volunteer for eco-causes*
- *Eat less factory-farmed meats and vegetables*
- *And anything else you can do to protect our planet!*

Be an eco-warrior every day by making conscious choices! The little daily decisions have a Compound Effect, as my man Darren Hardy says, so be deliberate with your everyday choices. You can make a difference!

The Trip of a Lifetime: Montana Mastermind Epic Camping Adventure

I know I mentioned it earlier but since we're talking Nature Connection, I wanted to share again with you a way you can tap into your primal self and and disconnect to reconnect with your higher self.

Picture hiking into nature's glory, over beautiful mountains, across rushing rivers, and camping out in the backcountry wilderness with a group of like-minded Happy Hustlers. We talk biz (specifically about creating more passion, purpose, and positive impact in your life), we crush primal workouts, take cold baths, practice deep meditations, learn primitive survival skills, study the art of fly fishing and much more... all the while epic lifelong friendships are created. In addition, we eat delicious healthy food prepared by a professional backcountry chef and get it all captured by a professional videographer and photographer for you to then leverage that content in your business later. We hang out around the campfire and tell stories and howl at the moon under the stars of Big Sky Montana. This is truly one of my favorite times of the year. It allows me (and everyone who joins) to completely reset while tapping into nature and our primal selves on a whole new level.

If you would like to learn more and see if it is a fit for you, head over to caryjack.com/montana and apply today. Spots are limited and life-changing fun is guaranteed. Yeehaw!

After roughly a 10 mile hike into the wilderness, we made it to one of my favorite lakes in the whole world!

HAPPY HUSTLER SPOTLIGHT

Yvon Chouinard

Yvonn Chouinard is an American rock climber, environmentalist, and outdoor industry billionaire. His company, Patagonia, is known for its environmental focus while giving back to the land. He is for sure a Happy Hustler and can often be found surfing off the coast of California or climbing in the mountains of Wyoming.

He is a master tinkerer and created the outdoor behemoth Patagonia back in 1971 by initially selling rock climbers more advanced handmade gear.

He has done so many wonderful things for this planet it would be hard to list his true impact in this short spotlight. He is connected with nature more than any billionaire I know of and does more for the environment because of his visceral bond.

Yvon is an amazing entrepreneur who has not wavered in his mission, and his company gives back 1% of every dollar earned to causes that help to protect and serve Mother Earth.

He is an avid fly fisherman (one of my all-time favorite things to do), climber, kayaker, adventurist, and indeed a Happy Hustler who knows how to balance nature, business, and the civilized world.

STORY TIME: NATURE AND YOUR HAPPINESS ENVIRONMENT

I heard the line screaming from my reel as I saw the massive bend in my fly rod. I had a monster trout on the line. After a long day's work (roughly 4 hours), I took off to the river to get some much-needed R&R. The river is my happy place, where I connect with mother nature and have a moving meditation in the form of fly fishing, forever searching for that perfect cast (although never achieving it). Immersing all of my senses in the glory of the pristine wilderness surrounding me, connecting with nature feels like medicine. And in order to Happy Hustle a blissfully balanced life, I must take my medicine on a daily basis.

I've lived all over the world, from Bangkok to Barcelona, from Rio de Janeiro to Buenos Aires, from Miami to LA, one place still and always has had my heart. That place is Montana. The reason I love Montana so much is because of the surrounding untouched nature. I moved here with my lover to build a life and a family. But more importantly, to connect with nature every day. Whether it's going on long hikes in the wilderness to remote lakes, or horseback riding in the open pasture on my trusty equine companion, or soaking my body at a thermal hot spring, this place and its majestic beauty had me at hello. Well, technically it had me since my dad moved up here when I was a boy. As mentioned, I split time growing up half on the beaches of Sarasota, Florida, and in half in the mountains of Red Lodge, Montana. Hence how I became what my friend Derek calls a "hippy cowboy".

After traveling around the world, I've realized that nature is missing in far too many areas for far too many people. The reason it is missing is that human beings have been destroying it. If it is missing in your area and in your life, maybe it is time you move. You need nature, we all do. If you aren't getting outside enough and connecting with Mother Earth, then seriously own it now and let's plan a change. I want blissful balance for you in your life but you have to be honest. And sometimes that honesty will lead you to a decision. A crossroads in which you must decide which path to take. As I did myself, while living in South Florida I knew I wanted more nature and fewer people. Sure, I would regularly go kayaking and fishing and bike riding and to the beach and to the state parks but even still it wasn't enough for me. My soul craves a self-sufficient sustainable ranch utilizing regenerative practices so that's exactly what I am planning to build. What does your soul crave? How do you want to incorporate nature more in you and your family's life?

ACTIONABLE TAKEAWAY

Ask yourself if your current environment possesses the level of nature you desire. And if not make a change. Now let me also mention, just so everyone doesn't up and attempt to move to Montana, that there are a ton of grizzly bears here that can eat you ;), and winters get down below -50° at times. This place isn't for everyone, but I do recommend you find a place that suits you and your family's natural needs.

I personally split my time between Montana and a tropical location during the wintertime (I like to pick new places). However, I make sure to get sufficient snowboarding shreddin' time in there. But to keep life interesting, instead of just buying a winter home in a sunny tropical place, I like to rent and explore other wild places that this beautiful Earth offers for extended stays. And I know since you are a Happy Hustler reading this book, hungry for a more balanced life, you may also be interested in splitting your time in multiple locations. If that is the case, heed thy message: don't settle. It is possible for you. Decide where you want to go and Happy Hustle to make it happen.

One of my favorite pics of me fly fishing at Lake McDonald in Glacier National Park.

EMBARRASSING FUN FACT

My brother and I once charmed the Director of Sundance Film Festival in order to gain access into the most exclusive event of the festival. It was a screening and live panel discussion for The Inconvenient Truth Sequel featuring Al Gore (Former Vice President and Climate Reality Founder), Robert Redford (Hollywood Star Actor & Sundance's founder), David Suzuki (TV Filmmaker of Nature of Things), Jeff Skoll (Founder of Ebay and Participant Media) and Amy Goodman (Founder of Democracy Now. All of whom we got to meet. We were ushered in like royalty from the Director of Sundance himself, Jon Cooper (great guy) and sat front front row. We learned about protecting our planet and networked with game-changing contacts for our company. All because of charm and persistence. A Happy Hustler always finds a way in.

EMBARRASSING FUN FACT BONUS

I once was dared in the wilderness to swim naked across a freezing river in exchange for $20. I got about halfway back from this ice-cold swim and my whole body locked up from the snowy ice-chilled water. I had to be rescued with a rope and to make matters worse as I was nearly lifeless, nakedly crawling up the shore, a Girl Scout troop was hiking passed on the trail. Yep, great timing…

POWERFUL RESOURCES

Books:
Let my people Go Surfing by Yvon Chouinard
The Practice of Natural Movement: Reclaim Power, Health, and Freedom by Erwan Le Corre

Podcasts:
The Happy Hustle Podcast, Episode 60, 68, 166
No Barriers Podcast with Erik Weihenmayer

Movie:
The Weight of Water

BONUS ALIGNMENT
BLISSFUL BALANCE

"LIFE IS LIKE RIDING A BICYCLE. TO KEEP YOUR BALANCE, YOU MUST KEEP MOVING." - ALBERT EINSTEIN

As you now know, **BALANCE = Happiness!** But balance is not a finite destination but rather a never-ending journey. It requires self-quantification, pivots, and adjustments along the way.

Reflect & Quantify

Balance is the not-so-secret to unlocking a life you truly love. One that legit overflows you with gratitude and emotion when you think about it. A life that fills you with joy. Let me just say congratulations on making it this far. I am super stoked for you. The fact that you're reading this right now means that you are well on your way to being a Happy Hustler. Keep going and finish strong!

See the key to creating and maintaining this blissful balance we've been talking about through this whole book is two things. 1) Measure yourself regularly in each of the 10 Alignments. Remember the S.O.U.L.M.A.P.P.I.N.™ framework? Yeah, measure yourself in each of those Alignments every Sunday evening (1-5) and use a Blissful Balancer fridge magnet every week to track your balance in real time… more on this below. 2) Give each Alignment (and its task) equal importance but FOCUS on one at a time. That means being fully immersed and present with the task at hand.

Be it a Zoom meeting for your biz (Impactful Work), a date night with your lover (Loving Relationships), or playing pick-up soccer with the guys (Passionate Hobbies), each task gets equal importance but should be focused on one at a time. See the problem is most people are thinking about their work when they are with their family and thinking about their family when they are at work, thus doing neither effectively nor being fully present in either. Don't let this be you any longer. When you are doing something, go all out and be there, fully immersed.

Now, at times, your life will indeed become out of balance, either one way or another. You may be working on a particular project with a time-sensitive deadline or training for a big race and all of your effort each day revolves around achieving the task at hand. It is essential to get back to a place of balance after those focused sprints. A place of harmony between your professional and personal life endeavors.

Ultimately, balance is a moving target. An evolving intangible goal. You can have it one day and then lose it the next. So how the heck do we find and keep it you may ask? Well, glad you asked. Like I said before, with the 10 Alignments and routine measurements mi amigo! I like to measure myself (1-5) every Sunday evening on the prior week's Alignments. I then prioritize change accordingly for the week ahead. That could simply mean just taking the quiz, www.thehappyhustle.com/assessment, or thinking about each alignment and writing down an honest score. Remember: what gets measured gets managed. And I highly recommend ordering (if you don't already have one) the Blissful Balancer fridge magnet to track the 10 Alignments and your unique Action Tasks each day. This will keep you accountable and focused on the key tasks in each Alignment while allowing you to track your balance and progress in real-time! You can get one at www.thehappyhustle.com/hub :) Now that you have some great resources to create and maintain that blissful balance in your life, let's dive into the 4 seasons of life!

The 4 Seasons

Just as there are 4 seasons in Nature, we can break our lives down in a similar fashion. Each season brings new challenges and objectives.

The seasons are marked not only by changing weather patterns, but by the stars, moons, and the sun. Native Americans knew the seasons of life and migrated their tribes accordingly. They knew when the bear would crawl into caves to hibernate that winter was near. They believed that when the eagle flies closest to the sun that spring is present. Native Americans were one with nature and respected the seasons.

Author's Note: It is a crying shame, an utter travesty, what many of our ancestors did (and still do) to these individuals. Now I am not naive to think there is anything I can do to right the wrongs or ease the pain suffered by these tribes and their people in the PAST, however I am doing my damnedest to give support and create a more unified FUTURE. And I hope you will too. We can learn from the Native Americans while honoring their culture and wisdom. One of the lessons I've learned is the importance of seasons.

With my Native American co-stars while shooting a documentary-series in Montana. Kind and professional, talented actors.

Many of our personal struggles and pains come from failing to recognize which season we are in. Swim upstream in the season when you're intended to flow downstream, and you'll be met with resistance and exhaustion. Flow with the current of the seasonal stream and accomplish your goals with ease.

Life is seasonal. In order to Happy Hustle a life full of Blissful Balance, you must identify: what season you are in right now?

Winter – the season of cold darkness where we reflect, regenerate, and rest.

Spring – the season of nurturing and budding greatness, a time of incubation and preparation.

Summer – the season to plant seeds, build, develop, hustle, and grow.

Fall – the season where you reap the benefits of what you sowed in summer.

By clearly identifying which season you are in, you can then release any unnecessary stress or pressure you may place on yourself and plan life accordingly. If you are in Summer and feel like you have been busting your butt, without much return, you can rest assured that Fall is just around the bend.

You will be rewarded for your hard work. Your seeds will grow and you will harvest your crop. Don't rush the process or dare to cheat the laws of nature and life.

If you are in Winter right now and are feeling a bit more anxiety and depression as to what your next moves are, allow yourself to rest and feel into

the season, don't fight it. Regenerate and know that Spring is near where you will learn, incubate, and prepare to unleash your greatness within. These individual seasons can last months or days, it truly depends. Some years Winter may be longer and harsher, while other years it may feel like a never ending Summer.

If we understand and apply the lessons of each season of nature, they will help us to have balance, peace, and happiness. Be deliberate with your actions in each season and know that the only true certainty in life is that change will happen. So, embrace the change my friend, and live each season to its fullest!

Out of Alignment

If you feel out of balance, you are most likely out of alignment in one way or another. There are always signs that show up when we become this way. Now whether we choose to "see" the signs and make a change is up to us. When a friend reaches out with constructive criticism, do you naysay their words away or do you embrace the feedback?

When you work tirelessly on a project and don't get the desired result, do you continue to plow forward or do you stop for a moment and reflect as to why it didn't pan out as you planned? When we are in alignment with our true purpose, it doesn't mean it's all rainbows and butterflies. There will inevitably be challenges and adversity to overcome in our lives.

However, when we are in flow with our higher calling (aka "in Alignment"), the answers will appear and we will do whatever is necessary to persevere. So, call it balance, call it alignment, call it flow, it really doesn't matter what the heck you call it, just create it and keep it as you Happy Hustle on your journey.

HAPPY HUSTLER SPOTLIGHT

Natalie Glebova

One of the first Happy Hustlers that comes to mind when I think of illustrating Blissful Balance is my friend, Miss Universe 2005, and UN Women's Advocate Natalie Glebova. She is not only a best-selling author, entrepreneur, and motivational speaker, but she is an amazing mother to her daughter Maya and wife to her husband Dean (also an impressively balanced Happy Hustlin' rockstar entrepreneur and friend of mine). They live on the beautiful beachfront in Phuket, Thailand overlooking majestic sunsets with crystal clear turquoise waters.

She is very passionate about empowering her audience to live life as winners while continuously improving. Using success principles, she's learned from some of her personal role models, such as Tony Robbins and Simon Sinek, Natalie became successful in many areas of her life including career, relationships, and personal fitness. She has launched her own brand of perfume BEAUTY ICON, runs a wellness blog HHB Life, is a best-selling author with her books *Healthy Happy Beautiful and I Am Winning - A Guide to Personal Empowerment*, and pursues her life-long passion for music by becoming a DJ.

As an avid entrepreneur, she co-founded an online startup called Travelbook with her husband Dean. It's a travel-sharing platform that connects travelers through their experiences (travelbook.com). Her current focus is on her online and offline coaching and courses that help others to be winners in life.

As a Russian immigrant who moved to Canada when she was just 13 years old, Natalie learned to overcome obstacles and low self-esteem as she was growing up in a new country and adapting to a completely different culture. It was with this strong mindset that Natalie chose to go for and achieve some pretty big goals - being the first immigrant ever to win the Miss Canada contest and ultimately winning the Miss Universe title in 2005. She's no stranger to barriers and Natalie possesses a winning mindset to set big goals and break through obstacles to achieve everything she wants in life - having a beautiful family, a successful business, and the freedom to pursue her passions.

Graduate of IT Management from Ryerson University in Toronto, Canada with a Bachelor of Commerce, she also has a certificate in Nutrition from Washington State University. Natalie has been very involved in charity work ever since she moved to Thailand in 2006, and was a spokesperson for worldwide and local organizations such as Habitat for Humanity, Operation Smile, SOI Dog Foundation, UNDP, WWF, and Freeland Org.

Natalie's philosophy is that every person has what it takes to live life as a winner, regardless of their current income, race, occupation, or relationship status. With the 7 winner's qualities, she describes in her book, each one of us can take our top place in the game of life.

Natalie is definitely a Happy Hustler who maintains Blissful Balance and if you want to hear more about her story, I interviewed her and Dean on The Happy Hustle Podcast episode # 29, check it out!

STORY TIME: I GOTS DA POO ON ME...

It was 4:00 A.M. in Amsterdam. I woke up to 3 inches of water soaking my clothes and a legit turd floating against my hair. Just an hour earlier, I had snuck into a shitty hostel room where my buddy was staying with 8 other people. I was broke and out of balance. I had no money to afford my own bed, so I had to sleep on the hard terrazzo floor underneath one of the bunk beds. Apparently, one of the dudes clogged the toilet and flooded the whole joint. My eye was swollen after getting in a bar fight earlier. You should have seen the other guys. I was sticking up for two girls who got sexually harassed by 3 men on the dance floor during a pub crawl. I also had just left the Red Light District. Needless to say, morale/self-worth was at an all-time low.

Don't let the smile fool ya, I was a hot mess at this time in my life. Sometimes in life, you learn the hard way, as I did in Amsterdam.

Just a couple of weeks prior, I thought I had had one of the lowest moments of my life after an all-night rager in Ibiza. Yes, the party island off the coast of Spain. I had fiesta'd at a foam party where they filled the club with foam from the floor to the ceiling and lost all of my money, phone, wallet, shoes... and dignity. I had been on an absolute bender. My body was run down. I was mentally spent. My sole focus at that time in my life was partying and women. Not necessarily in that order. Here I was, completely out of balance. Again, sleeping on the floor and covered in poo water with nowhere else to go. I realized that the last month in Spain had been a cakewalk compared to this shit - pun intended. Talk about one of the lowest moments of my life.

Were you ever so out of balance that a rude awakening shook you to the core? Well, this was exactly that for me. I knew I needed to change my ways. I knew I needed to become a better version of myself and start prioritizing what was important. I was far from home and very lost.

When you're out of balance, life has a way of letting you know. Sometimes, it will show up in the form of poop bobbing against your head. Other times, it may show up more slowly, in subtle ways. Regardless of how life lets you know you're out of balance, the point is that you can recognize it.

The first step to change is admitting it. I've done a lot of stupid shit in my life. Some of which nearly landed me in federal prison. One of which did lead me to be locked up in jail. Others led me to be held at gunpoint. Other acts landed me in the hospital. Others in detention. It took these lowest lows to realize just how high the highs have been in my life and this is what propels me to chase more of those amazing moments of balance.

Back in Amsterdam, I made a decision. I traded my life of imbalance and hustlin' for a life of balance and Happy Hustlin'. I traded crime and fighting for bliss and being the loving light. I traded partying and one night stands for prioritized reading and becoming a one-lover man. I was on a destructive path in my early years and would have most likely ended up in prison or worse. I know first hand just how sweet life can be with the proper framework and mindset. Both of which I hope you've learned in this very book.

The goal is that hopefully we grow from our mistakes and make different decisions in the future. Experiences are the best of lessons. Learn hard and learn fast, my friend. Or just learn from others. Hence, why I wrote this book. So, why not learn from my mistakes and avoid the angst yourself.

The 10 Alignments of a Happy Hustler can be a blueprint for building your dream reality. The framework you just learned is timeless. If implemented, it will genuinely provide you with the freedom and fulfillment that you desire.

ACTIONABLE TAKEAWAY

However, please know that balance is ever teetering like a see-saw. It requires constant tweaks, adjustments, and re-positioning in the form of honest introspection and daily inventory. I know it sounds daunting. But again, that is why I created the Blissful Balancer fridge magnet to easily quantify where you stand in your life in each of the 10 Alignments every single day. Tools like this parlayed with The Journey: 10 Days to Become a Happy Hustler online challenge can be your best friend while breaking old unbalanced habits. Remember, balance is a constant effort. Much like a tightrope walker, if they lose focus or stop walking while actively trying to stay balanced, they fall. Be active in your pursuit of balance. Be balanced in your pursuit of happiness.

EMBARASSING FUN FACT

I got two questionable tattoos under the influence. One in Bali on my ankle of a smiley face with a red x over the eye. This signifies that sometimes in life you get punched in the eye, but you can stay steady smilin' and persevere with positivity. Oddly enough, this little smiley later became the Happy Hustle logo. Who woulda thought.

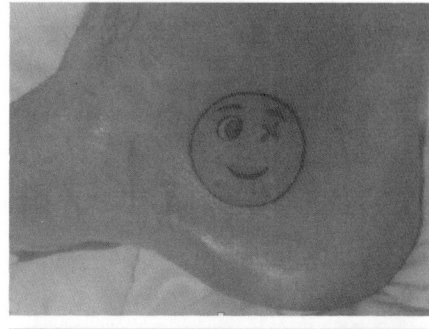
The notorious smiley ankle tat that started it all.

The other tattoo was done on my wrist while under the influence of Ayahuasca in the jungle of Costa Rica. It's a love and light bulb with a spiritual ankh symbol in the middle. Truthfully, it looks like a 10-year-old drew it. But, it signifies the transition from the darkness into the light. I now strive to always shine bright with love and light.

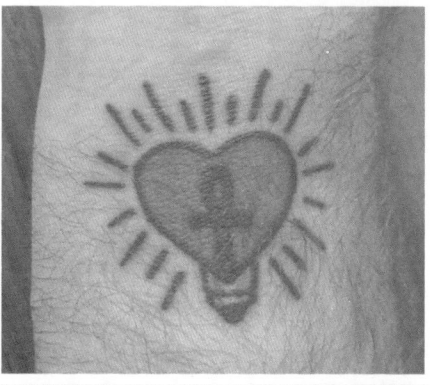
A constant reminder to always be the love & light.

POWERFUL RESOURCES

Books:
The Four-Hour Work Week by Tim Ferris
The Monk Who Sold his Ferrari by Robin Sharma

Podcasts:
Aubrey Marcus Podcast

Movie:
The Intern

Online Course: The Journey: 10 Days to Become a Happy Hustler (www.thehappyhustle.com/Journey)

BRINGIN' IT ALL TOGETHER

"I'D RATHER HAPPY HUSTLE 24/7 THAN SLAVE 9 TO 5."
-YOURS TRULY

IT'S TIME TO TAKE ACTION… THE HAPPY HUSTLER WAY

As this book is nearing its end, I want to impress upon you something. None of the pages you just read or the 10 Alignments you learned will matter if you don't ACT upon it. You must take action to become a Happy Hustler. You must adopt the mindset of a Happy Hustler and prioritize balance accordingly. As my friend and New York Times best-selling author Rory Vaden says in his book Take the Stairs, "It's not my right to tell you what you should do. I believe most of us already know what we should do. The problem is we don't do it. For most of us, it's not as much a matter of skill as it is a matter of will. Success means doing things you don't want to do. Action is the inevitable prerequisite for our success."

Man, does Rory nail it in that book which is a great read. If you haven't already read it, I suggest you do! But for real, you now have a choice to make. You can sit back and close this book after finishing these last couple of pages and go on with your life as it was. Sure, you can go to work tomorrow lacking purpose and do the necessary tasks as you have in the past. You can show up as you have been, not present or living each moment to the fullest. You can allow valuable time with your family and friends to come and go. You can procrastinate a little longer with your health and fitness goals and continue living less than your optimized self. You can put off doing your personal hobbies and having fun a bit longer. You can disregard Selfless Service and make helping others an afterthought that you get around to every now and then. You can continue to live unbalanced. But all of those choices won't get you where you want to go! They won't help you create your dream reality. They won't earn you the Blissful Balance that results in real, everyday joy. Those decisions will ultimately lead you to unfulfillment and a life of hustlin', but not happiness. There is another option…

You can take fucking action! You can say enough is enough. You can adopt the Happy Hustler's mindset and go all in. You can create a life of blissful balance full of passion, purpose, and positive impact! You can hold yourself accountable. You can be diligent with how you spend your precious time. money, and energy. You can take the assessment every week to find out where you're lacking and prioritize change accordingly. You can actually use the Blissful Balancer every day and track your real-time progress.

You can join The Journey online course to dive deeper and connect with other like-minded rockstar Happy Hustlers in an awesome Facebook group. Simply join "Happy Hustlers Worldwide". You can also hold others around you accountable and raise their level as you do your own. After all, we are all in this together. We can collectively make the world a better place. If you truly help others get what they want, you will ultimately get what you want.

I am so grateful that you gave yourself the time to read this book. It has been my absolute honor to share with you the 10 Alignments of a Happy Hustler and how to bake that blissfully balanced delicious life you love. (Oh no, not the baking reference again, Cary). To give you a recap on the recipe ingredients and a quick action reminder, it goes as follows:

1. **Selfless Service** – Give your time, money, and expertise to individuals and causes that you feel called to help.
   Happy Hustle Hack: *Schedule Giving.*

2. **Optimized Health** – Eat healthy, exercise daily, and stay disciplined.
   Happy Hustle Hack: *It's more important what you don't eat than what you do. Plus, stretch daily!*

3. **Unplug Digitally** – Disconnect to reconnect. 60 minutes in the morning upon waking and 60 minutes before bed. Be completely device free.
   Happy Hustle Hack: *Do 24hr digital detox on Sundays to recharge and start your week fresh and ready.*

4. **Loving Relationships** – Dedicate energy and attention everyday to those you love.
   Happy Hustle Hack: *If you want a 10, be a 10.*
   Plus, use a Love Calendar.

5. **Mindful Spirituality** – Have faith in a higher power.
   Happy Hustle Hack: *Practice daily meditation, breathwork, and gratitude.*

6. **Abundance Financially** – Increase your financial literacy.
   Happy Hustle Hack: *Create a system to spend, save, and invest your $$ wisely.*

7. **Personal Development** – Grow and evolve every day.
   Happy Hustle Hack: *Implement the 90-minute system for personal growth: 30 minutes reading in the morning, 30 minutes listening in the afternoon, 30 minutes watching in the evening - all inspirational and educational content.*

8. **Passionate Hobbies** – Have FUN doing things you enjoy regularly while prioritizing them with equal importance as work obligations.
   Happy Hustle Hack: *Do things you love to do minimum 2x per week.*

9. **Impactful Work** – Do something that excites your soul, something that infuses your passion and your purpose, and makes a positive impact while making you money.
   Happy Hustle Hack: *Figure out what problem you feel called to solve and who exactly you want to solve it for.*

10. **Nature Connection** – Connect with nature every day in some way, disconnect from your devices, and enjoy and protect Mother Earth.
    Happy Hustle Hack: *Commit to a 15 minute daily walk outside. Protect our planet by voting with your dollar and supporting conscious, sustainable companies.*

That is what this book is all about. The 10 Alignments is your path to the promised land. I'm telling ya, when I started implementing the Happy Hustle-Dote, the 5 Stages to Happy Hustlin', in each alignment and holding myself accountable in each, my life transformed and my happiness skyrocketed. The same will happen for you.

To recap, the 5 Stages to Happy Hustlin' in each alignment are how to transform a 1 ranking to a 5 in each alignment, here they are:

Apply The 5 Stages to Happy Hustlin' in each Alignment:

1) *Do an honest audit of your reality and feel gratitude for where you are.*

2) *Define your vision for success, what does a 5 look like in this Alignment?*

3) *Reverse engineer the process and create a winning game plan.*

4) *Take massive action and execute! Manage your time & priorities accordingly.*

5) *Persistent consistency. Enjoy the Journey Happy Hustlin' a life of passion, purpose, and positive impact.*

So wherever you're at in each alignment, you now know how to improve. When implementing all of this, the big thing is to push past the FEAR (False Evidence Appearing Real) that may be holding your transformation back. You know, that made-up story written by your mind, that's all fear is. **Want to know how you get past the fear? With action. Action is the cure for fear. And balance is the cure for avoiding burnout.** Even if you're scared or don't feel like it. Make the necessary changes. Take action!

I'm sure you're getting sick of me saying this by now, but I don't care because you need to hear it! I know I did. I needed that kick in the ass from my mentors and the books I read. And boy am I glad I got it. So, have the discipline to take what you've learned, implement it, and watch your life transform. Don't let fear hold you back any longer. Your time is now. The Happy Hustle is here to show you a better way to work and live, a way to have your cake and eat it too! A way to be balanced while in the pursuit of your goals and dream reality. A way to increase the freedom, fulfillment, and fun in your everyday life! Don't let this be the end, but rather just the beginning. Become the best Happy Hustler you can be.

To wrap up this book in style, I've got a couple calls to action for you. Links to everything Happy Hustlin' I mentioned in this book are on this page at www.thehappyhustle.com/hub. This hub was created especially for those of you reading this book, so you can navigate everywhere you need to go, not just once but regularly from now on! I would bookmark it on your devices. It is regularly updated with the latest Happy Hustlin' info, insights, tips, tools, and tactics to help you Happy Hustle your dream reality. You can go to thehappyhustle.com/hub or you can scan this QR code and dive right in!

Again, all the following can be found at www.thehappyhustle.com/hub. Here's a list of the action items, in order, I would do while on the page:

1. If you haven't already, take the **"Are you a Happy Hustler Assessment?"** This is a crucial first step.

2. Pick up a **Blissful Balancer fridge magnet** to measure and track your balance every day! Remember, what you can measure you can manage and this bad boy really helps as a daily reminder.

3. Next, join the awesome **Facebook group** and connect with like-minded rockstar Happy Hustlers from around the world. We are creating a movement together and this tribe's vibe is epic.

4. Join **The Journey: 10 Days to Become a Happy Hustler Online Course**. This is some of my best work distilled into a power-packed step-by-step course that helps you implement the 10 alignments and everything you just read into your everyday life!

5. Listen to **The Happy Hustle Podcast** for educational, inspirational, and entertaining episodes with some of the world's greatest Happy Hustlers!

6. Send the **FREE PDF download of The Happy Hustle E-book** to a friend in need. Spread the good word and help create more happiness in this world.

7. If you're an online entrepreneur and feeling froggy, apply to join **The Happy Hustle Club** to connect regularly with a tribe of Happy Hustlers who are crushing their goals! Get expert mentorship, gamified accountability, and an awesome community to help you Happy Hustle on your journey!

8. If you're a purpose-driven entrepreneur making over 6 figures per year and enjoy the great outdoors, apply for the **Montana Mastermind Epic Camping**

Adventure and see if it's a fit! Talk about one helluva good time mixin' business and pleasure in the beautiful backcountry wilderness.

9. There are a ton more awesome resources at **www.thehappyhustle.com/hub,** plus an amazing free Happy Hustle exclusive bonus that will rock your socks off. Check it out and see for yourself.

10. Final call to action, get out there and Happy Hustle *your* dream reality!

Use this link: www.thehappyhustle.com/hub to learn step-by-step on how you, too, can implement everything you have learned within these pages. You will find ways to take immediate action towards your happiness and become a Happy Hustler. There is also Happy Hustler swag, in case you want to rep the movement. You know a good hustler couldn't miss out on printing merch like dope hats, T's, etc. ;)

I truly hope you enjoyed the lessons, spotlights, stories, ridiculously bad jokes, Happy Hustle Hacks, and everything in-between. I have been truly blessed in this beautiful thing called life. There has been plenty of adversity along the way, much of which I left out as I felt it was not relevant to you at this time.

However, I do wish I had the foresight and knowledge that I now have. This is why I wanted to write this book and share the lessons learned along with Actionable Takeaways. My hope is that maybe, just maybe, if you are on the brink of burnout, hustlin' but not happy, or living a life of imbalance, that you will now be armed with the information needed to transform your reality. Within these pages, you have the power to create a blissfully balanced life that you love. I've offered you a system to infuse more freedom, fulfillment, fun, and financial abundance, which may lead to a life beyond your wildest dreams. The Happy Hustle is the way to the promised land and the Hustle-Dote is the formula.

Remember the **Happy Hustle-Dote**? Well, regardless of what you want, why you want it, and how and when you are going to get it, you can use this formula to achieve your desired results. It seems simple because it is. You can have everything and anything you want in this life. That is, if you're willing to hustle for it.

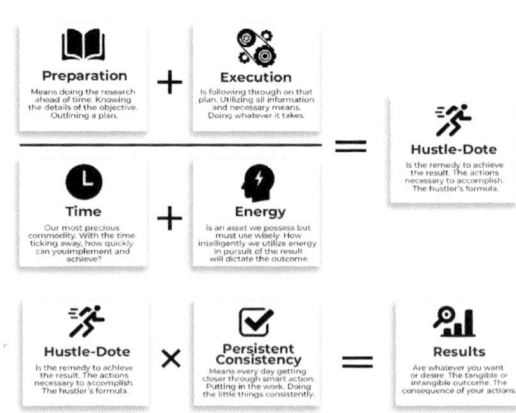

Willing to put in the sweat-equity. Willing to do whatever it takes. Hustle-Dote aside, my ultimate goal is for us all to find happiness and balance. I want to prove that you do not have to settle for what life gives you. You can create the life that you desire. With hustle, a clear vision, and a willingness to persist, anything is achievable. By deciding what you want and what you are willing to work for, you can begin the journey down the road of Happy Hustlin' to go get it while using the 10 Alignments to keep you balanced and happy within the hustle.

Again, it has been a real honor writing for you. From the bottom, top, and middle of my heart, I want to thank you for your time. Thank you for sticking with me page by page, reading my outlandish stories, and putting up with my cheesy jokes. Thank you for acknowledging my journey and learning how to Happy Hustle your own. I can hardly believe it is coming to an end. However, it's not goodbye, it's see ya later as I know a couple more books are coming your way in the near future. Stand by, my friend. To be honest, I now know what authors mean when they say writing is a "real labor of love". Holy guacamole has this damn thing taken love, energy, and focus on another level to finish it!

I can only hope and pray that my writing makes a positive impact on you in some way. This is an amazing adventure we are all on. Don't take a moment of it for granted. Life can change in an instant. So, love deeper, be kinder, and create balance.

Manifest your dreams and never stop Happy Hustlin', my friend.
I love you and am so grateful for you.

Get in, it's time to Happy Hustle baby!

Your friend and fellow Happy Hustler,

Cary Jack

"Time is the most precious commodity in this life so don't waste it!"

PS: Let's stay in touch and connect on Social at **@Cary_ _Jack!** If you see me on the street, come give me a hug or a handshake. I invite you to listen to my podcast, The Happy Hustle, which is available on all podcast platforms. Lastly, share your story of Happy Hustlin' at **www.thehappyhustle.com/story**. I love and appreciate you!

Stop flipping pages, and start Happy Hustlin' your dream reality!

More Legal Stuff

Copyright © 2021 by Cary Jack - The Happy Hustle

All rights reserved. No part of this publication may be reproduced in whole or in part, or transmitted in any form by any means electronic, mechanical, magnetic, and photographic including photocopying, recording or by any information storage and retrieval system without prior written permission by the publisher, except for the brief inclusions of quotations in a review. This work is intended as an aide to self-improvement only. This book does not seek to give medical advice and is not a substitute for licensed medical care. Readers shall hold harmless the author and publisher for any events or actions that arise from the reading of or attempts to implement the methods in this book. Neither is any liability assumed for damages resulting from the use of the information contained herein. Note that this material is subject to change without notice.

ISBN: 978-0-578-97719-5

Cover Design by Jason Lefrock, Studio 217

Edited By: Charles Serabian & Megan Kendzior

Happy Publishing INC

www.TheHappyHustle.com

Thanks again for reading!

Peace & Love.